BAD BIZ

Your Guide to Starting a

For-Profit College

(A Satire)

Corin Devaso

Copyright © 2019 JV

Bad Biz is an independent project for educating the public through creative writing and satire. The authors of *Bad Biz* are professionals who have worked in the industry or business described; they may also be professionals with a keen understanding of the inner workings of the bad biz. It is the responsibility of the reader to research the business to determine opinion from fact.

This book is not to be used as an actual guide for starting a for-profit college. This book is satire for the purpose of educating the public about business schemes and scams.

To contact the author, feel free to reach out through social media.

Before we begin...

This book is satire but the situation is very real.

For-profit colleges (and some non-profit institutions) have been scamming students for decades, leaving hundreds-of-thousands of students with massive debt and no degree nor job training to show for their expense and time. This widespread fraud has devastated communities and families...and it continues unchecked and rarely challenged by the politicians elected to protect our youth.

Please help new and prospective students by sharing this book on social media by using the hashtags **#CollegeFraud** and **#CollegeScam** in your next post. And if you would like to be bold and take it a step further, tag your state senator on the post or share the link for this book with your state's department of education and/or senator.

With average graduation rates dangerously low at these particular colleges (anywhere between 15% and 35% graduation rates), the scam cannot continue any longer.

Thank you

Table of Contents

Preface 4

Chapter 1: The Essence 6

Chapter 2: What is a For-Profit College 13

Chapter 3: Sources of Revenue 31

Chapter 4: The Organization 50

Chapter 5: Marketing the Myth 75

Chapter 6: Admissions The Gateway to Destruction 85

Chapter 7: Retention: Keep and Plunder 101

Chapter 8: Programs and Curricula 119

Chapter 9: Accreditation: Legal Extortion 131

Chapter 10: Compliance: The Fishing Guide 139

Chapter 11: Ignorance Pays 146

Chapter 12: Customer Service: Reselling the Dream 152

Chapter 13: Support 160

Final Advice 166

Preface

Bad Biz is a business satire with two purposes: to reveal to the reader how nefarious businesses evolve and thrive, and to alert the public to businesses that exploit everyday people. The author of the book has experience working in the business or industry written about, so you're getting a first-hand account of what goes on behind the scenes.

It should also be noted that the information in this book does not apply to one specific company or organization. It is up to the reader to take the information in *Bad Biz* and research the facts. Again, this is satire to educate you, the reader, about devious business. The author is writing from the perspective of a fictional tycoon with an unscrupulous character. However, in real life, the author is a professional or whistleblower who wishes to alert the public to his or her previous experiences with bad biz. This particular book is about for-profit colleges, and the author worked in the for-profit college industry.

If you believe you're currently being exploited by the type of business written about in this book, then it's encouraged you break off that relationship and seek professional advice.

Satire is a fun and creative way to learn something, but it can also be crude and offensive, so proceed with caution. In no way should this satire be used as a real guide to starting a for-profit college. Our hope is that from having read this book, you will be better equipped to protect yourself and your community from a nefarious business.

Chapter 1
The Essence

Did you go to college, and did it leave you with a load of debt? If you're like most graduates, then you have a degree, or perhaps a few degrees, but not the income to clean up your student loans. But if you've never attended college, then you haven't been suckered... yet. The college dream is an effective hoax that makes student loans appear attractive and drives countless dimwits into debt, like a rite of passage into bona fide adulthood. Wouldn't it be amazing to start a business that profits off student loan borrowers? Whether or not you've been caught by the student loan trap, you can make a fortune from it. This book will show you how it's done.

At the outset, it's important to weed out any noble ideas you might have about *success*. Underachievers define success in terms of happiness, contentment, emotional fulfillment, helping others, security, love, blah, blah, and blah. This book isn't about such superficialities. It's about achieving real success, which is the drive and determination to become a financial rock star. To reach this goal, I'll focus on a cunning manipulation of the college myth. As a warning, the tone of this book will challenge you to drop any illusions you have about success, as those illusions will only get in your way of accomplishing the ultimate goal of vast wealth.

If you continue to hold onto ethical values and beliefs, unable to depart with strong morals and convictions, then you'll have difficulty learning the lessons in this book, and you'll remain a middle-class schmuck. However, if you wish to become incredibly rich, join an elite group of profiteers, and live in an affluent and secure euphoria, then you must eliminate all virtues and commit yourself to a business that destroys vulnerable lives. This book will help you do just that, by teaching you how to start a for-profit college.

A deception relative to the one aforementioned is the myth that says a college education increases a person's income by millions of dollars over a lifetime. You may have heard this fabrication before. I hope so, for the purpose of this book.

Believe it or not, it's true: a college education can dramatically increase your income, but not in the way you may be thinking it would. I'm not talking about your college education. Instead, I'm referring to the education of those simpletons who still believe the American Dream is possible, start from severe disadvantages, are susceptible to false promises, and can be easily exploited for your financial gain. I'm talking about the college education of the most defenseless people in our society.

This book will show you how to start a for-profit college that sells the mythical dream of success to the poor lambs who thirst for a better life, while giving absolutely no guarantee or intention of providing them with a quality education. If you desire sustainable wealth without guilt, this book will be more valuable than an MBA from Harvard. The best part is that you don't even need a college education to start working this lucrative scam.

In essence, this book will assist you through the process of starting a for-profit college without disgrace, regret, or remorse. It'll help you become so wealthy that the doors of opportunity will never close. You'll start multiple businesses, buy an island in the Caribbean, wine and dine with powerful politicians, get elected to office, be regarded amongst world leaders, and establish a network of powerful and rich people. You'll far exceed expectations by legally exploiting lower- and middle-income buffoons who truly believe a college degree is an answer to life's problems.

Did I mention you don't even need a college education to pull this off? All it takes to start your for-profit college is ambition, information, and the ability to replace a moral compass with an appetite for profit. This book will prepare you for the journey.

By starting a for-profit college, you'll be entering into a largely untapped industry with little regulation. Unlike the businesses of healthcare and real estate, higher education is like the Old Wild West — it's still new territory with criminals running wild, robbing, and pillaging federal funds. Education laws are so vague that regulators don't understand the policies they've written to protect students and taxpayers. Law interpretations vary widely, and most of the enforcement depends on the current political party at the helm.

With for-profit college revenue flowing mostly from federal loans and grants, this is great news for anyone with the acumen to start and run a for-profit college business. However, it's still important to understand postsecondary education regulations, as there are a few of them you must follow to operate a viable business protected from damaging lawsuits.

Don't be intimidated. As you'll learn throughout this book, many laws that are meant to safeguard student borrowers will benefit your business indirectly. You'll have to play the regulation game to earn big, and this book will help you do just that.

This book will also help you employ the right people. Employing the wrong crew can lead to a devastating end. You'll learn to employ people with weak moral compasses, who are incredibly desperate for a job or simply too naïve to understand the nature of your operation. Frontline workers will be representative of your customer base, living paycheck to paycheck, and will respond favorably to fear-based micromanagement. Besides, some of your employees will be students at the college, so you can see the effects of your scam in action as they work tirelessly to pay off the debt that you have saddled upon them.

You'll also learn to pick upper-level leadership with great care. One slip-up, such as placing a highly ethical person onto your leadership team, might put you in a world of trouble very quickly. We'll discuss how to take great care in choosing your team and much more.

As you're reading this book, the words "students" and "customers" will be used interchangeably. Remember that your endeavor is, first and foremost, making a profit. Actual education is a far second, or perhaps in fifth place. Students are simply customers who feed the revenue stream and supply ridiculous amounts of profit through federal aid.

Throughout this book, you'll be taught how to identify and target your customers. Topics such as enrolment, retention, marketing, financial aid, regulation, compliance, accreditation, organization, shareholders, and other business-related essentials will be covered to help you start-up without anxiety. If you're wondering why the topics just mentioned don't include areas specific to academia — such as college preparedness, college readiness, academic assessments, best practices, or remedial services — don't worry.

Let's be clear: you don't need to be an educator, know anything about postsecondary education, or embrace any ethical philosophies related to academic achievement.

A desire to help your customers obtain a quality education at an affordable price will only hurt your venture. For-profit colleges are in the business of making a profit, not helping students reach fanciful goals. If this bothers you, please question whether or not you have the temperament to become filthy rich.

As you may have already noticed, the terminology in this book might appear harsh at times, but it's important to become desensitized to the destruction that your business will cause in the lives of students and their communities. There is no escaping the reality. You may come across terms such as "victims," "saps," "suckers," "idiots," and "fools." These terms are always referring to your customer base, and sometimes to your employees.

Remember, a moral compass will point you to failure, so this book will continuously test any nobilities you have that can threaten the success of your lucrative for-profit college.

Follow the lessons in this book, work hard, and you just might become crazy rich. Starting a privately owned for-profit college is a sure way to become a financial success.

Let's get started…

Chapter 2
What is a For-Profit College

For-profit colleges get a lot of news coverage, but most people don't know what they are or how they make their money. Students attending for-profit colleges are often unaware they're enrolled in a private counterfeit operation; while graduates become aware of the scam after being routinely turned down for jobs. Not many businesses want to hire for-profit college graduates, except for-profit colleges.

Global ignorance of the for-profit college industry is one of your greatest assets as a nefarious entrepreneur. The less is known about private for-profit colleges, the more money you will make in the short term. As their name suggests, these specific colleges are inherently for-profit, not for-student. Let's go more in-depth.

A for-profit college is a privately owned, profit-seeking business. Notice how terms like *academic institution* or *public* are not part of the definition? By nature, for-profit colleges are not concerned about the best interests of students or the communities in which they reside. Before you commit to starting a for-profit college you must understand that these specific colleges are not established for the betterment of local communities. The purpose of this collegiate enterprise is to exploit hundreds of suffering communities for profit; perhaps even tens of thousands of communities, depending on the scope of your operation. Don't be ashamed. Most of these communities are in shambles anyway.

Keep in mind, your goal is to start, own, and eventually sell a profit-generating machine that extracts subsidies from the rat-holes of society and converts the aid into great wealth for the most important person on the planet…you. Though you'll be exploiting low-income communities, you'll be wise to give your college a name that appears representative of a community – perhaps using the name of a state or major city, but strictly for branding purposes.

The alternatives to for-profit colleges are non-profit colleges in the form of traditional institutions, such as community colleges, faith-based schools, and state universities. Perhaps you're a proud graduate of one of these alternatives. Some people argue that the traditional non-profit schools craftily funnel as much money from impoverished communities as for-profit schools, but in more subtle ways. Presidents and deans of state universities have salaries comparable to for-profit college CEOs and CFOs; and the amount of funding state colleges spend on their athletic programs is astronomical, if not criminal, in comparison to what's spent on student services and faculty development.

Even faith-based institutions rob students by charging outrageous tuition for degrees holding no practical value in the job market. Isn't there a commandment about not stealing from the poor and naïve; and wasn't there a wise man who said something like, *"Serve the poor and needy"*? That's where your enterprise will come to the rescue - to serve and save the destitute who've been turned away by expensive and discriminatory non-profit colleges. For-profit colleges brand themselves as the saintly savers of all who've been rejected by traditional universities. Wearing this halo will make you rich.

Your business will be offered to low-income, marginalized, and hurting populations as an alternative to the non-profit schools. The average for-profit college customer won't have the intelligence, ability, or funding to attend a traditional college; but he'll still want a degree because he believes it's necessary.

Ever since childhood, the average for-profit college customer has been told, *"If you want to amount to anything in life, you must go to college. You can be the first college graduate of our family, and perhaps you'll become president of a big company someday. You can be our winner in a family of losers. It's all on you! You're the chosen one."* Millions of struggling children hear this message every day, and this makes for a constant supply of desperate suckers who scramble to meet arbitrary expectations. As such, the supply of prospective customers is so huge that there aren't enough colleges to enroll all of them.

Even community colleges, which have very low graduation rates, are turning away students for lack of space, resources, and teachers. Thus, for-profit colleges are a salvation for people unable to attend college through traditional means. Your business will rescue people deserted by non-profit institutions; and then you'll take their abundant financial aid, letting them drown in their own debt. We'll talk more about that later.

The Critics:

If you have the guts, acumen, and chicanery to launch a for-profit college, you must understand the ethical arguments made against your mission. Critics of for-profit colleges vomit all kinds of nonsensical attacks:

> *They're only concerned about profit, not student success or outcomes. They charge way too much tuition for useless degrees. They target minorities, specifically African Americans, for their access to federal loans and grants. Most of the student loan defaults in America are made by for-profit college students. Only a few students graduate, and not many find meaningful employment post-graduation. For-profit colleges intentionally target*

military soldiers and veterans for their access to Department of Defense funding. The Admissions Departments are essentially boiler-room sales offices pressuring people into starting academic programs they cannot attend nor afford. They do not assess for college preparedness and enroll people who cannot read or write. Most of their revenue is from taxpayer dollars, but without a return on investment for the taxpayers.

These are just a few of the arguments made by civil rights advocates, special interest groups, and students who've been bamboozled by for-profit colleges. Later on, we'll discuss how these arguments have validity and can help boost business.

Don't forget, this book is meant to prepare you for starting a successful fraudulent business. Let's not sugar coat anything; instead, let's accept the realities. If you try to debunk the critics to justify your intentions, you'll lose your mind and abandon the venture. Don't attempt to convince yourself and the critics that you're a good person offering a service to the destitute of society. Stay focused on profit-making, not attacking the critics.

The arguments against for-profit colleges have a lot of legitimacy. Most of them are true. But your job is not to fight them. Your job is to understand each critic's perspective, respond appropriately and professionally, and make loads of money from students who are not already paying for a traditional college education.

When you must respond to critics, keep it simple. Effective responses used by successful for-profit colleges sound something like this:

> *By being a for-profit college, our motive is efficiency; and by being efficient, we can offer the most affordable quality education to people who never had the opportunity to attend college. We offer them the freedom to choose their education and let them have control of their destiny. We trust the adult student is capable of making the best decision in light of her life's circumstances. We offer her what traditional schools have failed to provide. We only profit if the student succeeds and is proud of her education. When non-traditional schools have turned her away, neglecting her needs, we have embraced her. We openly accept all people, because we believe every person has the right to an affordable and quality education."*

Learn this response by heart, study it, and ensure that every employee you hire is trained to accept this duplicity in the depths of their souls.

Corporate Affiliation:

Though you may be starting small, many of the for-profit colleges in existence and thriving are subsidiaries of large corporations traded on the open market. This might appear to be a conflict of interest, and that assumption would be absolutely correct.

For-profit college students rarely realize their school is owned by a publicly-traded corporation. Just this morning, a middle-aged guy in his underwear traded a for-profit college with a few taps and a click; and none of the students were aware of his transaction. The wealthy day trader has no problem playing with the school's stock, and he certainly doesn't have the students in mind while trading them like cheap baseballs cards. The trader's ignorance exists for good reason.

The parent companies of for-profit colleges do not want traders and shareholders pondering the real and devastating impacts on student loan borrowers. Profit wouldn't be as plentiful if traders fairly understood how the school's stock price impacts a single mother working three jobs and taking out thousands of dollars in unsubsidized student loans. It's best for the shareholder, and ultimately you, if that struggling mother is represented as a simple data point on an attrition chart provided to investors. So, if you ever become large enough to trade on the public exchange, be happy when casual day traders traffic your students for monetary gain. But these greedy basement traders aren't the only ones playing with hot for-profit college shares; and this, again, is good news for you.

Many for-profit college shareholders and traders are much bigger players than the successful day trader. Hedge funds, retirement funds, big banks, and massive domestic and international financial institutions are amongst some of these giants, to name a few. The for-profit college companies add a unique flavor to large investment portfolios. Wouldn't you want to be the next spicy addition to a firm's portfolio? If you can prove your business is a high-risk investment with some level of stability and predictability, you'll become filthy rich within no time. This isn't a book about investing, so you can look up the fancy investment terminology later, but be aware that many for-profit college companies offer a wonderful midsized and small capital option to portfolios with values in the billions.

The option for-profit schools provide is attractive because the risk is high; so there's potential to make huge gains. Contrary to what you might assume, investors don't look at graduation rates to determine investment quality; instead, they look at enrollment and attrition data when deciding to buy or sell a for-profit college company. If enrollment numbers appear to be suffering, they sell. If the college reports an increase in new students for the quarter, they buy. This is one reason why graduation is not important to for-profit colleges. It just doesn't matter to the company, traders, and shareholders if a student graduates. As this circus of investing occurs, the students are unaware their education is being traded like silver coins amongst greedy profiteers.

Perfect Solution:

For-profit colleges have always been in the business of making entrepreneurs very wealthy. Decades ago, savvy entrepreneurs found an opportunity to profit off the G.I. Bill when first introduced as a veteran's academic grant. These profiteering geniuses started vocational schools as a way to absorb the G.I. Bill, marketing their programs as the perfect solution for returning soldiers to obtain civilian job skills. Later on, the Higher Education Act (HEA) was established by the federal government and inadvertently allowed for-profit colleges to receive federal funding through its *Title IV policy.*

Pay close attention, because the federal Title IV policy allows you to receive all types of subsidized and unsubsidized loans through your customer base; and the policy also kicks back money to your students for additional expenses. This additional funding is a natural incentive for low-income borrowers to enroll at your for-profit college. How can these poor saps pass up free money? Well, it's not necessarily free, since taxpayers are constantly replenishing federal student aid funds.

Think about it from your customer's perspective: attend class and receive a few thousand dollars on the side to use freely. Your students will use the extra funding to pay electric bills and rent, or gamble and pay bail. For-profit colleges have the perfect client demographic to be reeled in by HEA grants and additional funding. You don't even have to explain to customers the difference between subsidized and unsubsidized loans. Remember, they're adults and should be figuring out those debt traps before signing the enrollment agreement.

As a for-profit college owner, your primary responsibility will be making a profit off students' access to government loans and grants, not offering financial aid advice or safeguarding them from debt traps like your own. Though you're building a business from their entitled access to funding, the federal government does not expect you to be an honest fiduciary; you'll be the complete opposite. The for-profit college business is a venture of taking, not giving – unless you consider the giving of lifelong debt an act of generosity.

Even though you'll have access to taxpayer dollars through HEA funding, the Department of Education has a cap on the percentage of revenue that for-profit colleges can launder through taxpayers. That cap is currently 90% - this is fantastic news for you. That means only 10% of your revenue has to come from sources that are not federally funded; such as private loans, student payment agreements, and the Department of Defense.

With 90% of your revenue streaming from a source almost guaranteed not to dry up, you'll be setup to prosper. For-profit colleges must be doing something right because their students cause most of the student loan defaults in postsecondary lending. In other words, you are entering a business that is very lucrative at the expense of the students, government, and taxpayers. Fingers will be pointed at your school for the amount of money you siphon from taxpayers without producing anything of real value to society, but you can easily point your finger at the HEA policies and tell your critics the system is setup for you to take advantage of taxpayers and low-income borrowers.

For-profit colleges are essentially asked to participate in the grab for federal funding. If it's allowed and legal, why not play and profit? If the federally regulated revenue cap ever fell from 90% to 70%, or lower, then your business would be in trouble – in that case, you would need to find a way to make up the missing 30%, and you know your students won't be able to afford tuition out-of-pocket. For-profit colleges need that revenue cap to be as close to 100% as possible; your entire business will be dependent on those federally-funded student loans. Thankfully, the laws governing access to those funds should be around and unchanged for a very long time, and there will never be a short supply of suckers taking out student loans.

As is mentioned repeatedly throughout this book, for-profit colleges target specific student populations, and these groups are your bread and butter as they unknowingly hold the key to vast reserves of federal funding. Your job is to steal the key.

Target Customers:

It's important to understand the types of people who are eligible for federal grants, such as the Pell Grant. Low-income borrowers are eligible for the Pell Grant, which is just one of the blessings bestowed on us by the Department of Education. This may be a good opportunity to assign you some homework, so you can learn about the lifestyles and characteristics of your target customers, especially how they communicate.

Take a few days and drive through the worst neighborhoods closest to you: public housing areas, trailer parks on the fringes, poor rural communities, dangerous urban centers, minority neighborhoods, flea markets, courthouses, casinos, half-way homes, addiction clinics, etc. These are just a few areas you should visit. Spend some time studying the people. If you're brave enough, walk the streets and converse with the residents. Get an idea of what they want from life and what skills they're lacking.

Take detailed notes, paying attention to how they communicate with the world. These communities and their struggling residents are the backbones of every successful for-profit college enterprise.

Get creative and visit rehab centers, homeless shelters, methadone clinics, mental health facilities, and nursing homes. All of these places have people who are isolated, depressed, and are thirsty for a solution to their life's terrible circumstances. Remember, you'll be offering a solution, whereas the traditional universities offer these people rejection and judgment.

Over the decades, for-profit colleges have mastered the art of manipulating low-income borrowers into enrolling and staying enrolled. This mastery is due to an expert understanding of the stresses and conditions these people live with. As a result of this understanding, for-profit colleges have collectively made billions of dollars by offering hope, convenience, and location. Since many for-profit colleges operate mostly online, which offers the best location and convenience, students simply need access to the internet to enroll and attend.

This common need for online convenience will provide you with an easily subsidized revenue stream. Imagine that, a tap on her Smartphone and you can log a student's attendance and start banking off her funding; and with every update of the student's attendance, she will receive additional funding to support destructive financial habits. It's a win-win. The student receives additional funding in the short-term, and you receive her entire allotment. Let's leave out the part where the student's debt catches up to her, she defaults, train wrecks her family, and causes a colossal student debt bubble in our economy.

Going back to the life circumstances of your average customer, many for-profit college students don't own a car, have lost licenses, or just don't have the time or ability to drive to an actual building. It's more appealing for these people to attend an online program; and an online platform allows you to charge higher tuition than community colleges, without the costs of building space and maintenance.

Besides the convenience of being online, for-profit colleges also advertise the convenience of flexible course schedules at paces that fit the lives of non-traditional students. However, you make more profit by convincing students to attend on a quicker paced schedule - the faster the pace, the faster the revenue stream, thus the greater the profit. Remember, you're not in the business of helping a deadbeat graduate; however, you are in the business of siphoning student loans into your revenue stream as quickly as possible.

A Few Selling Points:

We've come a long way from the commercial vocational schools that for-profit colleges were first disguised as. Today, we don't have to provide relevant skill-based education to students interested in entering the workforce or changing occupations. The reality is some mook will mortgage his house to get an MBA in Marketing – a useless degree that'll make your business spike. The old idea that a college degree is essential for success has leaked down to the most vulnerable and desperate populations in our society. Just watch day time or late-night cable television, it's littered with for-profit college commercials drawing in thousands of people.

As a nefarious entrepreneur, the benefit to you is that a college degree can now be obtained entirely online. No need to start a vocational school with labs that teach nurses to draw blood, mechanics to turn wrenches, or X-ray technicians to zap injured limbs. Those types for vocational for-profit schools still exist in brick and mortar structure, but it's easier to establish an online program that only requires Wi-Fi connection. For-profit education is primarily online and flourishing. In fact, traditional schools are consulting for-profit colleges to create online degree programs of their own, since the for-profit colleges have mastered the online format. Mergers are happening between for-profit and non-profit schools for this reason. Greed does prove to benefit actual postsecondary education after all, but on a small-scale.

Another great selling point for the for-profit colleges has been the caliber of adjunct instructors with *real-world experience.* You'll want to incorporate that term into a few marketing campaigns. People who are unable to attend traditional schools do not like feeling inferior, and for-profit college entrepreneurs have picked up on this important fact. As a result, they have developed a message difficult to ignore. It goes something like this:

> *You will be taught by expert instructors who are currently working in their professional fields. They will teach you real-world lessons and skills that you can apply immediately. Don't settle for boring professors who are out of date; instead, network with the most qualified professionals in the real world. Enroll today!*

This message invites the non-traditional student to feel empowered and supported by a college that will accept him with open arms. It's important to understand this point: Your prospective customers feel defeated because they were unable to attend a state school; but they'll feel lucky to have found you as the perfect solution to all of their problems, of which there are many. Put yourself in the students' shoes, which some of them won't have because they're dirt poor. They are living hopeless lives, yet they can be given access to real-world professionals who might open doors of opportunity.

Professors at for-profit colleges do actually work in their designated fields of study, but they're not necessarily experts or effective teachers. Most have not even taught a course at a traditional school. We just figure our enrollees won't know the difference between effective teaching and someone who follows pre-made lesson plans designed by paid consultants.

Not all for-profit college professors are inadequate teachers, but the ones that are intelligent, skilled, and ethical tend to quit quickly once they've realized the predatory nature of the business. Even when the professors don't measure up to student expectations, automated teaching programs make the online programs appear legitimate. Adaptive learning programs are being used by for-profit colleges to help students grasp lessons in mathematics and the sciences, and these automated programs are a great selling point to prospective customers. A customer can work through automated lessons at his own pace without stressing over weekly assignment deadlines.

Despite the benefit, what the customer doesn't know is that the online adaptive learning systems exist to update his attendance, not for learning new skills. Whenever he works through one of the automated lessons, his attendance is generated and this allows you to obtain and hold his federal funding, which is dependent upon attendance. So, the best approach to selling the quality of your online program is to highlight real word professional faculty along with automated lessons that allow a student to work at his own pace. In actuality, most of your student population will fail at any pace, but you get the idea.

Hopefully, by now you have a basic understanding of for-profit colleges. You'll pick up much more in the coming pages. If at any point during this book you feel disgusted with the content, it may be a great time to put it down and reflect on whether or not you have the tenacity to start this profitable journey. A lot of money can be made in this venture, but you must be able to stomach the realities behind the revenue. It's not recommended that you justify reasons for starting this business. You'll likely lose the college if you do.

As mentioned previously, simply embrace the beast. Become what you want to be – a filthy rich for-profit college tycoon who exploits countless suckers eligible for federal funding. If you spend time and energy fighting the remnants of a moral conscience, you won't have the ability to run a for-profit college the way it is meant to operate.

Chapter 3
Sources of Revenue

The primary source of for-profit college revenue is none other than your government; and to be more specific, the taxpayers who fund the government. All the working adults you see daily pay taxes, and a portion of those taxes are allocated for federal student loans and grants. So shake your neighbor's hand and thank him for supporting your new enterprise. Wait a second, hold off on shaking anyone's hand for now. It's probably best to keep this fact unrecognized until you've made off with as many of their tax dollars as possible.

Try not to boast about your venture to taxpaying neighbors and relatives; you don't want your loved ones knowing you exploit poor saps for profit. Your parents, spouse, neighbors, and employees should have no clue you're funneling their tax dollars into your for-profit college business. Ultimately, they are the source of your revenue, so treat them well and keep them clueless to your chicanery.

Don't broadcast this truth to prospective students either, and don't fool yourself into thinking you're making money from non-federal sources. If the federal government puts a stop to its free-for-all student loan program, for-profit colleges will fail quickly. Your security lies in the reality that the federal student loan program won't change soon or quickly, and it will always offer taxpayer dollars to naïve hopefuls underprepared for a college education.

Eligibility to Receive Federal Funding:

Accreditation, which we'll talk more about later, allows you access to the deep pool of federal student aid. Once your college becomes accredited, you're then eligible to receive Title IV federal loans and grants with little government oversight. In other words, accreditation is your license to steal.

The trick is obtaining accreditation, but there are easy ways of doing so. Savvy for-profit college entrepreneurs often seek out small accredited colleges that are failing, perhaps on the brink of bankruptcy and desperate for financial relief. They'll then purchase the small suffering school, with its accreditation, for pennies on the dollar. Think of it like this: If the student aid revenue stream has a dam holding back its golden rivers of wealth, accreditation is the release valve. Because accreditation can be tricky to obtain when starting, you will be wise to find failing accredited colleges with the release valve open, in need of rescue, and desperate to believe their original mission and values will be honored after the transition.

When you find an accredited non-profit college that fits your budget, convince its leaders that you'll keep the college's original mission, buy it, and flip it into a profit-making machine. If you are successful in purchasing a small accredited college, don't forget to terminate the employed remnants of the institution. You'll need to bring in droves of boiler-room workers whom you can properly train to administer your larceny.

Accreditation is not your only tool to access taxpayer dollars. There are many federal policies in place to help you secure eligibility to receive funding. A Higher Education Act policy called *Ability to Benefit (ATB)* allows you to receive federal funding from an endless supply of buffoons, especially the academically unprepared pool of illiterates. The ATB policy was initially implemented to ensure student loan borrowers are using our tax dollars appropriately. It's a safeguard to prevent wishful thinking students from spending tax dollars on failed courses and multiple attempts of a program. This might scare you, considering your business will focus on the exploitation of low-income borrowers; however, don't let it.

The ATB policy, along with accreditation, works in your favor. This is a great example of how a federal policy meant to protect taxpayers and students can benefit for-profit colleges instead. The loopholes are wide and plentiful. Keep in mind that you are in the business of finding and using federal and state loopholes to your advantage. That's the game.

ATB requires non-accredited schools to implement a college readiness test to enrollees who don't have a high school diploma or equivalency. With regard to accredited for-profit colleges, the ATB policy simply requires students to prove completion of a high school education before receiving federal aid. So, you'll only need a copy of the customer's high school diploma or transcript to start taking their student aid. You won't need to test for their actual ability to succeed in your school. To make more money off this loophole, you can give students until the end of the first term to submit their proof of high school graduation, but charge them for the classes they've attempted.

If a student doesn't have proof of high school graduation on file by the end of the first term, you'll have to administratively withdraw her for not complying with the ABT policy; however, you can still require her to pay tuition and fees for the first term. It's an unethical trick, but the student should have realized that a person needs to complete high school before moving onto college. Thankfully, there is an endless supply of suckers who don't know the rules. At the end of the business day, the uneducated and ignorant are your bread and butter.

You might be thinking, "*Is that it? I only need to prove that my incoming students have a high school diploma or GED! Who doesn't have that? Didn't they account for the countless people who've finished high school with extremely poor results and special accommodations? Didn't they consider the poor quality of our city and rural high schools? What about the adult student who's forgotten basic math and cannot write an essay to save her life?"*

It's amazing to consider that all you need is a copy of a student's high school diploma or transcript to take her Title IV funding, but it really is that simple. Point the finger back at your critics and tell them this is the law, and you're following it. It's totally legal. Not ethical, but legal. If you were ethical you wouldn't be profiting off regulatory ambiguities.

It's because of governances like accreditation and the ABT policy that your college doesn't have to be a diploma mill. It's not worth the risk to push students toward graduation. For-profit colleges don't profit from graduating students. Vague regulations support your college as an open enrollment school that doesn't need resources in place to educate at-risk students. Do you know how much revenue would need to be allocated to academic resources and support services to help the average for-profit student graduate?
Forget the nonsense of helping an inarticulate adult reach graduation; it'll cost you too much, and your profit margins will suffer. Plus, what will a graduate do with a degree from your college? Embark on a professional career journey? Considering the low academic quality of for-profit colleges, you won't want many

of your graduates in the job market. You also don't want a loss in future revenue as a result of thousands of graduates proving to employers their college education was counterfeit. It won't look good for the graduates, and it certainly won't help you grow your customer base.

At some point in your business development, you might want to expand into large corporate partnerships, so protect your reputation by producing very few graduates. To maintain a strong revenue stream, it's paramount you focus on admission and retention, not graduation.

If the Department of Education ever musters the audacity to question your low graduation rates, point them to their ATB policy and say, "*Hey, you asked me to ensure my students have the ability to benefit. Here are copies of their high school diplomas and GEDs. I acted in good faith.*" But don't worry about government scrutiny if the political winds are blowing in your favor. The for-profit college industry has always done favorably under certain administrations.

For reasons beyond this book, certain political parties have lobbied and supported the for-profit college industry as a model of profitable private business. The irony is that there isn't a return on investment for taxpayers or students. The for-profit college industry is well hidden from the masses and traded like a black-market drug. Let the rivers of federal funding flow wild and free.

Pell Yeah:

As mentioned, Title IV funding will be an essential source of profit; but even more specifically, the Title IV Pell Grant will have a significant influence on your bottom line. The Pell Grant was established to subsidize the education of people who cannot afford tuition on their current salary, or lack of. To be eligible to receive Pell Grant, a student must have serious financial needs and have never completed a college program. To continue receiving this free aid the student must maintain active enrollment - meaning the student must continue submitting class work regardless of quality.

Think of it like this: If an impoverished student submits a blank assignment through your school's online portal, you can receive and hold his Pell Grant funding as revenue and ultimately turn the aid into profit. There's no oversight concerning the quality of his work. What's important is his actual assignment submission for attendance purposes. Without the poor man's weekly online attendance, you won't receive the thousands of dollars his Pell Grant is worth. Wondering how you can get a homeless person to submit an online assignment so you can retrieve his Pell Grant? We'll discuss those methods later on.

Many low-income students can accrue thousands of dollars in Pell Grant per year; this is a huge incentive for them to attend your school. Pell-eligible students will enroll and apply for federal student loans simply to receive additional funding through stipends. It's a win-win: you receive the federal student loan payments, while they receive funds to be used for a weekend shopping spree. In reality, it won't be a long-term win for the student, as they'll end up with massive loan debt in the future; and very possibly defaulting.

Remember, you're no one's big brother. You can't stop Pell Grant abuse from happening. If they don't use your business to obtain and abuse the free aid, they'll use someone else's for-profit school to benefit. It's important to point out that not all Pell-eligible students enroll to gain additional funding to purchase the newest big-screen television or support other terrible spending habits. Some students simply fall into the Pell trap after tasting the fruit of additional funding. Your goal is to enroll as many Pell Grant eligible students as possible, get them to taste the sweet stipends, and let them drown in debt.

To continue receiving the students' federal loans and grants, every student must complete a new FAFSA (*Free Application for Federal Student Aid*) annually to determine eligibility. Think of the FAFSA as an application each enrollee must complete to determine debt capacity. The more debt they're eligible to accrue, the richer you become.

Dedicate an entire team in your Financial Aid department to contacting students who have approaching FAFSA deadlines. If a student doesn't submit his FAFSA form on time, the government may not approve his loans or Pell Grant. This will remove any incentive the student has to continue taking classes at your college. Do you think the majority of your students will continue taking courses if they lose their loans and grants, which they'll depend on for rent, childcare, and lottery tickets?

You must stay on top of students' FAFSA deadlines for this reason. If your students lose the Pell Grant, they won't continue taking out student loans; thus, you will lose them as customers. As soon as you start the for-profit college enterprise, direct your departments to call, text, and email new and continuing students who must submit their annual FASFA. Hound them until the submission is complete. Send daily reminders. It'll appear you are interested in protecting their best interests, but in reality you need for them to complete the FASFA accurately and on time.
Many students will need information from old tax returns to complete the FASFA - as you can imagine, a portion of your delinquent students will not have filed taxes for years, so strongly encourage them to contact the IRS to resolve tax issues. If prospective enrollees appear lazy or uninterested in contacting the

IRS, tell them they won't be able to attend college without their tax returns on file, and will thus end up dying alone and poor without achieving their dreams. There are so many creative lies you can use to ensure students submit the FASFA on schedule and solidify financial aid. The bottom line: You need all customers to complete and submit the documentation needed for a government-approved FASFA. Your business depends on this.

Once a student completes her FASFA and becomes eligible for the Title IV Pell Grant, she can then receive Pell allotments for up to six years. This is also great news for you. A student who attends your school for six years will generate much more profit through the Pell Grant and accompanying federal loans than a student who graduates early or on time. For this reason, you will benefit most if students do not complete your program. A program extended and not completed is worth more to you than a program completed early or on time.

Later, we'll discuss the importance of implementing policies that ensure your students stay enrolled regardless of academic performance. Again, if you keep students enrolled by any means necessary, and keep their FASFA updated annually, the sky is the limit for the amount of profit you can generate.

Widen the Stream:

It will also profit you to know about the *150% Rule*. This is a rule enacted by the Department of Education that doesn't allow your students to attempt more than 150% of their total program credits. That's the equivalent of a student failing or withdrawing from half of his courses. This 150% rule is meant to protect taxpayers from footing the tuition bill of Pell Grant recipients who have no intention of graduating.

So for example, if your Bachelor of Science in Business program is 180 credits, a student cannot attempt more than 270 credits in that specific program. If she attempts more than 270 credits, she'll lose federal funding; but it shouldn't matter to you since she has spent an enormous amount of tuition on incomplete courses up to her dismissal. Remember, a program extended and unfinished is more profitable than a program completed successfully and on time.

If you would like to squeeze more funding from a student who violates the 150% Rule, have your Retention Department transfer her into a different program before reaching the maximum attempted credit limit for the original program. If the Retention Department is unable to catch her before the 150% Rule is violated, have your Re-entry Admissions Department contact and return the student into an entirely different and meaningless program. Simply convince the ignoramus that a Criminal Justice or Psychology degree is more in-line with her career goals. Why should she go for a business degree anyway? Tell her everyone has a business degree nowadays, so Psychology will appear more unique to an employer. Tell the pushover anything to keep her, and her Title IV eligibility, active. The longer you hold onto her, the more money you make.

Create a new dream for the student using a new program, and let the funding gates open wide once again. Your Admissions and Retention Departments will be masterful in the art of creating dreams for your hopeless little lambs. The greatest Retention Advisors will instinctively transfer students from one program to another until the students have reached their aggregate loan limits. The average student's loan debt will be enormous, but so will your profit. By playing this transferring game, you'll profit more from one futile customer than three successful graduates.

Anything you can do to widen the school's revenue stream will be in your best interest: You don't want to graduate too many students; and considering the students who do graduate, you'll want to re-enroll them into additional programs. It's best to convince students to accelerate their program pace so they're taking more courses and paying more tuition every quarter, but it's even better if they're retaking classes or switching programs. Don't provide costly academic resources; however, retain your active student population at all costs. Let them naturally fail or withdraw from your program. Never intervene for their best interests, and never willingly let them withdraw to save themselves and family from surmounting loan debt. This approach allows you to receive tons of federal tax dollars from their ignorance, but also allows you to place blame on the student for not meeting programmatic expectations.

The for-profit industry is about sales, and the selling doesn't stop after the enrollment agreement is signed and federal funding secured. As we'll talk about later, the selling continues regularly to prevent students' federal funding from being returned to the government.

Federal Loans:

About federal student loans, you'll want your students to borrow more than they need. Encourage loan addiction. The average for-profit college student will trust that your Financial Aid Advisors are protecting her financial interests. It's comical but true. Your Financial Aid Advisors should be speaking optimistically at all times; never promising nor guaranteeing loan amounts, but speaking hypothetically to give the victim hope that her tuition will be fully covered - including the multiple failed course attempts and surprise fees sprung randomly throughout the enrollment period.

Since it's mandatory that you review with the student her federal loan rights and responsibilities, such as her responsibility to pay back the loans, do so vaguely by offering a multiple-choice entrance exam that can be repeatedly retaken. The student can continue taking the loan counseling exam until she memorizes the answers, or a Financial Aid Advisor can review the questions with her and assure her she'll be admitted. You simply need to show regulators that you tried your best at warning incoming students about the potential pitfalls of taking out student loans.

Remember, your Financial Aid Advisors should be trained to encourage students to complete the FAFSA hastily and begin using federal loans despite inherent risks. If an enrollee is intelligent enough to question loan risks, the Admissions Advisor can tell the prospective customer, *"Of course loans are a risk. But don't we all have to take risks on our road to success? Unless you can afford our tuition charges out-of-pocket, you'll have to take some risk. How will your life change if you don't take a chance, especially on something worthwhile, such as a college education? You owe it to yourself to enroll. Sign these documents."* Few students will question the risks, but train your frontline Admissions Advisors to respond appropriately if they're faced with an inquisitive enrollee.

After the customer takes the bait and completes the FAFSA application, the government determines her financial need. At traditional universities the student population consists of people with various financial needs; but at for-profit colleges, the need is always on the high end. Most of the students will be eligible for student aid; so the majority of their loans will be government subsidized, which is a great selling point to prospective customers. Unsubsidized loans require the student borrower to pay interest as soon as the loan is approved, but subsidized loans don't require as much payment from the student since the government covers the interest while she's taking classes or delaying payments. But there are caps on how much money student borrowers can receive from subsidized loans, dependent on tax status.

At some point the average for-profit college student takes out a mix of loans – subsidized, unsubsidized, and private. Why would someone take out a variety of student loans you might wonder? The answer will be: You're an amazing for-profit college tycoon, your Admissions Advisors can sell like pros, and low-income borrowers tend to get addicted to loans and additional funding.

However, it's not just about receiving federal funding, but as importantly…keeping it. If you're unable to hold the student's funding, then you would have to return revenue that could've been used to enroll additional suckers and market your brand. There is another regulatory rule called *R2T4* (Return to Title IV) that you can use to keep student loans in your revenue stream. *R2T4* requires accredited colleges to return federal funding that has not been used during a break or withdraw period.

The bottom line: Keep the students enrolled and attending so that Title IV disbursements do not have to be returned to the government via the *R2T4* rule. If a student demands to withdraw from the school, for something such as a death in the family or medical emergency, offer him an option to stay active at the university without having to withdraw entirely. If he withdraws completely, the funding is returned via *R2T4* and you lose out. To keep his funding in your pocket, this Title IV regulation requires the student to provide written confirmation that he agrees to return for the next scheduled course. To stay compliant to this rule, simply provide him with a form he must sign to confirm his return to the next session and assure him you'll hold his place in the program without forcing him through a re-entry enrollment process.

It doesn't matter if he returns to the next scheduled course. The point is to hold the funding and use it as revenue while he's taking care of his sick wife, burying a friend, or serving a prison sentence. You can also incorporate a tuition charge for dropped courses during the term. It's a triple win for you: The student pays for the dropped courses, he also pays for the retake of the courses, and you don't have to return his funding to the government. Do whatever is necessary to keep from having to return federal funding to the government. We'll come back to this lesson later.

<u>Military Gold:</u>

Apart from securing Title IV funding, there's a special maneuver that will boost your profit margins substantially. People tend to assume American soldiers, active and non-active, attend college using free federal funding. Not necessarily. There's a widely unknown fact: Military funding is not considered federal funding supported by the Department of Education. Soldiers and veterans who wish to utilize military funding, such as the G.I. Bill or Post 911 Grant, are not using federal student aid. Why is this important for you to know? The answer lies within a federal regulation called the *90/10 Rule*.

The federal government established the *90/10 Rule* to protect taxpayers from being cheated by scandalous colleges. The rule allows for-profit colleges to receive up to 90% of revenue from federal student loans; the other 10% must come from non-federal student loan sources. So, military grants are incredibly beneficial to your bottom line, because they can be included in the 10% allowance.

This oversight means you can grow the profit margins by millions if the Admissions Department enrolls soldiers, veterans, and military spouses. Isn't that great! Hopefully, the government won't change the *90/10 Rule* any time soon. As of now, military funding is like a huge bonus to for-profit colleges. Aggressively sell your college programs to anyone associated with the military, including military spouses who are also eligible for military grants. By doing so, you'll increase profits and receive even more federal funding from the 90% allowance.

Military students eligible for military grants and funding are like precious gold, so treat your military students especially well. It's like your military students are serving you twice. As mentioned previously, don't let a moral compass knock you off course. Start military-friendly campaigns at your school, start or donate to a wounded soldier fund, or hire active military and veterans as advisors or instructors. Hiring veterans will be a great addition to your brand and a marketing ploy that indirectly increases enrollment.

Consider adding the term *military-friendly* to your marketing repertoire. You can even offer a scholarship to wounded veterans, but keep it limited to a handful of military students. As with your general student population, it's not like you'll be spending much revenue on resources and services to help military students. All things for profit - remember this first and foremost. The goal is to offer a service that appears helpful and essential but is incapable of doing much good. Students and front end employees will believe you have a good heart by serving active soldiers and veterans. This false image supports your brand and keeps the revenue stream flowing.

Chapter 4
The Organization

The top leaders at for-profit colleges are typically recycled within the industry and for good reason. Traditional schools wouldn't dare hire a college president, dean, or provost who worked for a sham college that manipulated students for profit. For-profit college leaders are always 100% profit-driven; thus, their ambitions wouldn't be well accepted at traditional schools; just as you wouldn't hire an academic professional who puts students' best interests before profit. Would you want a campus president who implements policies that prohibit exploitation? Absolutely not!

Of course, there are academic regulations that need to be adhered to, but the goal of your leadership team is to ensure the business is growing, not slowing down because of a fruitless dedication to educate people. Ensure the leadership of your organization understands the government regulations, identifies regulatory loop-holes for manipulation, creates in-house policies and procedures allowing for the exploitation of student finances, abides by state employment rights, and can be trusted to keep inaccurate data concealed.

Some prominent for-profit colleges have been forcefully closed for reporting false data, such as enrollment and job placement rates. You'll indeed be operating a business of pure carnage, wreaking havoc on the financial futures of students and their families, but you must ensure your leadership is not tempted to report false data to the Department of Education or related regulatory agencies.

Choose Wisely:

When hiring suitable leaders, you'll need people who fit the mold. Focus on salespeople, preferably who've worked in industries that are heavily regulated and shady. With experience navigating complicated regulations, these experts can see past the red tape and identify opportunities for expansion and growth. Scout out leaders who've worked, or are currently working, at other for-profit colleges. As mentioned, the for-profit college industry recycles top talent; however, be advised to carefully research leaders at competing for-profit schools. You don't want to hire someone who's currently under investigation by authorities for falsifying data, which is common; nor should you hire a leader who doesn't have a network of sharks to back the chicanery.

If you do find a suitable administrator at a competing for-profit college, offer the person a competitive compensation package, or make the majority of the compensation dependent on revenue growth. These professionals understand that profit is the name of the game, not academic achievement. Like you, they're in it for the money and desire to be filthy rich.

By offering the leadership team a decent base pay and an even more impressive profit-sharing incentive, you'll ensure they stay the course and focus on financial growth instead of student success. It's human nature to satisfy and succeed, so if your leadership team wants to be rewarded well, they must do everything possible to produce a profit; and they will. If a dean position candidate tells you he believes profit is a byproduct of student success, such as high graduation and job placement rates, you can consider him for the position despite the ethically sound appearance. Simply showing up to the interview is a sign he cares absolutely nothing about student success rates or student loan defaults. By saying profit is dependent on ethical outcomes, what he's conveying is that he knows what to tell regulators if ever questioned about false data or complaints. This would be a good candidate for a second interview.

If a different candidate for the dean position tells you he is ready to steal every penny from the poor souls sucked into your enrollment trap…turn him away. This particular candidate is being too obvious and can be a risk to the company if ever reviewed by regulators. Hire leaders with tact, who speak the academic lingo of the regulators, and can play the part. Despite the second candidate's accuracy of the operation, he doesn't have a filter and might brag about your predatory endeavors to mooks at his local pub; the next thing you know, the bartender happens to be a student and reports you to the Department of Education and Better Business Bureau. Even worse, the bartender spreads word of the encounter on social media or posts a video of the drunk and bragging dean online. The next thing you know, *#predatoryschool* is getting a lot of followers. It's better to hire leaders who do not have a moral compass yet have tact and common sense to appear ethical. It's about the image.

Keep Your Leaders and Front-End Separated:

Whoever you hire onto the leadership team, make sure they don't have much interaction with your bottom level employees. Keep the leadership team away from the day-to-day operations of admitting, retaining, and manipulating students. Bottom level employees will eventually become burnt out and frustrated.

Front-end workers will often question whether or not the school is helping low-income students improve their dreadful circumstances. If upper-tier leadership is regularly interacting with employees at the bottom of the totem pole, their time will be consumed by responding to employee complaints and frustrations as those emerge. The next thing you know, you'll have a leadership team that is also burnt out and frustrated; or even worse, questioning the mission. Keep the majority of the anger, dissatisfaction, and ethical concerns at the bottom of the chain - amongst the advisers, teachers, and mid-level managers. Once a quarter, conduct a large forum one hour in length, where employees can ask questions. This outlet will give them the idea that you care about their success, as well as the students.

Train and prepare your leadership team to address common front-end employee questions such as:

> *"Our students are failing and withdrawing at incredible rates. Less than 30% of them are graduating. What are your plans to increase graduation rates?"* or *"My assigned students have a severe federal loan default problem. I know we can't suggest that a student withdraw, but how do I protect my students from taking on debt they can't pay back?"* or *"We haven't received raises, but we're expected to enroll more and more students. What's the incentive to enroll more students without receiving more compensation?"*

These are smart questions, and whichever Admissions Advisor asks that last one, find a non-discriminatory way to fire that employee. The leadership team must be prepared to answer such questions vaguely and confidently, and be able to deal with potential threats, such as the smart employee who asked about enrollment incentives.

The incentive for all lower rung employees is to simply keep their jobs, which is enough incentive since your front-end workers will be from the same low-income demographic as your students. The desperate enroll the desperate.

Political Connections:

It'll be wise to find leaders who have friendships with politicians, lobbying organizations, and companies with a strong interest in for-profit education. One might question: Why would anyone in politics have an interest in persuading low-income borrowers to attend a sham college? The answer is: Because for-profit colleges generate a lot of money and have found a savvy way to absorb taxpayer dollars on a massive scale. This money can be shared with politicians, who in turn support policies in favor of keeping you in business without harmful regulations. It's a network of financial abuse that is surprisingly legal and has multiple players.

So, you should pick leaders that: understand this network, have previously profited from it, and can boost your standing in the game. Consider what companies directly, and indirectly, benefit from for-profit education, and recruit leaders from those affiliate companies. Debt collection companies, asset recovery businesses, and lenders are a few of the players that can offer you an appropriate leadership team. Recruit leaders who personally know managers in the for-profit education sector, can successfully market and sell a worthless service, and are adept at manipulating frontline employees with charisma and business acumen.

Non-disclosure:

Every leader you hire should sign a non-disclosure agreement to keep your company's secrets in-house and to lessen the risk of having a pesky whistleblower on your team. For-profit colleges are organized similarly, but someone on your team might create a new marketing strategy, software, or discover a niche market that hasn't been previously tapped.

As an example, let's imagine the Vice President of Marketing discovers an increasing demand amongst elders to return to college, and as a result sets up a marketing campaign to recruit older adults from retirement communities, nursing homes, and dementia care centers. This is an example of information you don't want to be passed on to a competitor. As another example, the head of your Technology Department may develop an app that automatically reminds students to update online course attendance by easily posting a word or symbol; such a developed idea can help you get ahead of the curve and absorb more federal aid than competitors.

Since competition is continuously searching for ways to manipulate student attendance, you'll need to protect software developments by having your entire technology team sign non-disclosure agreements. Most of your business will be online, so fully protect your developments.

Leaders Know that Students are Numbers:

With for-profit colleges driving the evolution of online academic platforms, it's critical to ensure your team is up-to-date and aware of the newest software that can generate student attendance. Getting students to attend courses, especially online, is key to your success. During retention efforts, your leadership team should be responsible for getting every department, including the Financial Aid Department, involved in pressuring students to attend class. As we'll talk about later, the bread and butter of your operation is heavily dependent on student attendance.

The leadership team should be stressed and struggling to think of ways to coerce students into updating attendance every week. This challenge will keep them up at night with nightmares of losing hordes of students to dreaded regulatory attendance barriers. This leads to another important point: Your organization should always view students as numbers, not real people with actual lives and families.

If your leadership team has direct and frequent contact with students, the business is in danger of failing. The college's president, dean, provost, ombudsman, and directors should have minimal contact with actual students. Let's be real, even if you pick the most immoral leaders who've bartered a moral compass for profit, they're still vulnerable to empathy and sympathy. And so are you! So, be careful that you and your leaders are not in direct contact with the student population, except for the few students who attend graduation.

Do you want to listen to a struggling student rant on and on about needing to withdraw from the school to focus on his health, finances, or family? Do you want your dean talking to a homeless woman who's failed ten courses because she doesn't have a computer or shelter? Do you think the provost wants to listen to a veteran with PTSD complain about how the college doesn't offer remedial services to assist him with Algebra? With a high percentage of disabled students unethically enrolled by your Admissions Department, and retained by your Retention Department, do you want anyone on the leadership team having regular contact with these depressing realities?

The students represent one thing: profit. Regularly exposing leadership to such sad human beings would only destroy your mission, purpose, and drive. Remind yourself that leadership is made up of individuals with emotions, and for that reason, you must keep leaders from interacting with the general student population. Keep their moral compasses at bay. That goes for you as well! This is how you'll maintain focus. This is how you'll become crazy rich in the for-profit college industry.

Students are numbers, not people. Repeat that over and over to your leadership team. Bombard your team with charts and graphs that show enrollment rates, retention metrics, attendance barriers, attrition data, FASFA submission numbers, and anything that can numerically represent students. There's a reason why a rancher doesn't name his cattle and the farmer doesn't name his dog. For that same reason, you don't want the executive team forming relationships with students. That would be preposterous. Your Admissions Department should have digital counters, viewable from every area of the office, showing the number of students being enrolled hour by hour, as well as the number of enrollments that must be met to meet budget.

The Retention Department must also have queues and counters showing how many students have yet to update course attendance, and showing how many have requested to withdraw. You're not in the business of forming relationships with students. You're in the business of transforming desperate lives into cold numbers, measured and analyzed for profit.

The more data collected on your students, the better informed you'll be to maneuver the operation. Just don't share the data broadly, especially not with the lower-level employees working directly with students, regulators, or the public. The data you are required to share with regulators needs to be filtered and refined to tell a successful academic narrative, not the true story of student failure and debt traps.

The Board:

If your business grows large enough to have a Board of Directors, then it'll be critical to keep the Board participants unknown to employees and students. The purpose of the Board is to make pertinent decisions regarding the financial health of the company. For this reason, keep the Board in the dark and unfamiliar with issues that might affect their moral conscience. Ensure they're aware of positive student outcomes and narratives only. If a Board member becomes aware that the Admissions Department is using high pressured sales tactics to reel in vulnerable single mothers and minorities, you might have some explaining to do. Then again, whoever is on the Board of a for-profit college should be intelligent enough to know the business involves a great deal of exploitation and deception.

It may be beneficial to include members on the Board who've started non-profit organizations. For one, it makes them look good; and secondly, if the college is forced to shut down after an investigation, then perhaps the Board member's non-profit organization can absorb the assets. You can then rebrand as a non-profit college contracting with for-profit student services, which perhaps you'll have invested in.

Hierarchy:

The structure of your organization should have the most important departments at the top of the hierarchy. Marketing and Admissions Departments are at the peak. The majority of your revenue will be allocated to keep these two giant departments healthy and viable. The Retention Department, typically known as the Student Success Department or Student Advising Department, is a close second in importance. Retention is an extension of Admissions, so the Retention Department should be fully staffed and led by people who think like enrollment specialists.

Next in line within the organization will be Student Support Services - typically these are smaller service departments focused on matters related to academic success, but are not that important since academic services are far removed from the revenue stream. Student Support Services include areas such as Registrar, Prior Learning Assessment, Financial Aid, Career Services, Graduation Committee, Online Campus Support, Library, and Tutoring. You might be thinking, *"Financial Aid? Shouldn't that department be higher on the hierarchy?"* Not necessarily.

Financial Aid indeed is a critical department, so you can place it below the Retention Department in priority, but don't confuse the Financial Aid Department with the student aid pilfered from naïve dreamers. The college's Financial Aid Department exists to field general funding questions, manage students' FASFA submissions and deadlines, ensure funding limits are not reached too soon, follow federal guidelines involved in returning Title IV, and to send students to your Admissions and Retention Departments. Even though the entire operation is about enrolling and retaining low-income borrowers, your Financial Aid Department should be focused on regulatory issues only.

If you fudge any financial aid records, keep funds that should have been returned to the government, or don't follow the federal government's instructions, you can be put out of business along with being sued. Keep all of your connivings in the Marketing, Admission, and Retention Departments; but keep the Financial Aid Department clean, for the most part. If you want to squeeze a bit more profit through the Financial Aid Department, then play dumb. For example, simply explain to regulators that you weren't aware that holding vast amounts of Title IV money for an extra week would be problematic.

You may have noticed departments like Faculty and Career Services are on the backburner. Not entirely, but that would be an accurate observation. Most of your faculty should be adjunct and uninvolved in university operations. Professors will manage courses with occasional quality control assessments to meet regulatory guidelines. As you grow, you may hire thousands of faculty members - as many as you wish, since they'll be auxiliary without benefits. Adjunct faculty members will be teaching online courses to put extra cash in their pockets, and they won't need strict oversight.

With regard to the Career Services Department, it needs to be in existence for accrediting purposes and will act as a great marketing tool during enrollment. Admissions Advisors can frequently highlight the Career Services Department as a ploy to convince enrollees that your business cares about career development post-graduation. Vulnerable goofs will simply enroll because there's a Career Services Department, which they'll naively assume will find them a job or internship. By reading this far, you should be aware that very few of your students will make it to graduation; and even fewer will graduate and obtain a meaningful career in their intended field of study.

The Career Services Department needs to be staffed with low-level employees who are trained to spew gibberish sounding like market research, supply outdated job searching and interviewing tips, and provide resume and cover letter assistance to graduates who still can't write properly. Remember, your focus is on making a profit. It's a waste of your time and revenue to ensure graduates obtain careers that provide the public with positive returns on tax dollar investment. Hopefully, your Career Services Department will be the most hated department by your critics, since you're using taxpayer dollars without producing skilled workers to replenish the government's funds. The more blame that is placed on the Career Services Department for not helping your graduates, the more attention is taken away from the critical operations of your ingenious scam.

Human Resources:

As the owner of a for-profit college you'll be sued, and probably a lot. Being sued is a sign of success in this industry; however, to prevent frivolous lawsuits eating into your bottom line you'll need to establish a topnotch Human Resources Department capable of deterring behaviors that jeopardize the enterprise. The misconception that Human Resources exists to protect workers' rights may be true in ethical business, but you'll be operating a for-profit college. In your situation, Human Resources protects the company first. Like many of the college's business operations, you'll need to disguise the true intention of Human Resources by shaping it around state and federal guidelines.

Let's say there's an employee who relentlessly questions your business ethics, such as marketing to homeless veterans with access to military grants. You can discharge that numbskull in an at-will employment state, which many states are, without giving a reason; but why risk a retaliation lawsuit? Instead, use the Human Resources Department to find a legally justified reason for terminating that person's employment. Attendance, performance reviews, excessive breaks, misreporting data, questionable manners or hygiene…the list of reasons to fire someone is long.

It might take a few weeks to a few months to carefully execute the conditions for termination, or implement new policies causing the conditions, but it's better than opening up to public scrutiny during a lawsuit. Just remember to discard or cover up any in-house communication related to unethical treatment of your terminated employees. Emails, instant messages, and text messages should be deleted if they can lead back to the mistreatment of an employee.

The best way to go about nefarious terminations is to conspire behind closed doors with management and a representative from the Human Resources Department. With this said, your management team should be trained and ready to scout for legitimate reasons to fire employees, even employees who are not a current potential threat. The best approach is to be proactive in case any employees, especially the tenured ones, decide to veer from the mission and follow their moral compass toward whistle-blowing. Rats are everywhere, so choose a director of Human Resources with the expertise to lay and set the traps.

Whistleblowers must be trapped and discharged, so Human Resources will need to be vigilant while preventing the usual offenses that can harm any organization; so, set in place Standard Operating Procedures addressing serious claims such as sexual harassment and race discrimination. Never forget, you're aim is to be a profit-generating monster disguised as a legitimate and ethical business; so it's imperative to take a zero-tolerance stance on common workplace offenses. Though operating as a destructive force, you'll still want recognition as a safe employer. Set procedures in place to address and eliminate employment complaints that can prove to violate state and federal labor laws.

Using a comparative analogy, imagine your for-profit college operation as a methamphetamine lab. There's no doubt meth is a drug of devastating effects, and we know it shatters the lives of countless victims. The drug lab boss knows this fact but stays focused on the mission. The drug lord keeps the operation spotless, uncontaminated, and free of frivolous meth technicians. The villains responsible for running the meth lab follow the rules, remain professional with one another, and understand the importance of keeping a clean and uncluttered environment. Similarly, you'll need to operate the tax laundering business by federal and state rules, despite its devastating effects on the public good. No matter what positions they fill, you'll need to fire the employees who put the operation at risk of investigation for senseless behaviors. You don't want the entire Admissions

Department investigated because the Director of Admissions was sleeping with every attractive employee who couldn't meet quota. By setting strict operating procedures to exterminate the rats and roaches, you'll maintain a clean workplace that drives attention away from the bigger picture of profiting off vulnerable borrowers.

Employee Recruitment:

One of your greatest assets will be an employee recruitment team made of specialists masterful in screening and interviewing clueless candidates. The recruitment specialists will be well adept at identifying what types of persons will be successful in the enrollment and retention roles. Most job candidates will be oblivious to the real nature of your hustle. Job descriptions must be written to attract intelligent candidates, but not candidates who are too intelligent or overqualified. Being there are different types of intelligence, the recruiting specialists should focus on job candidates who are street smart, not book smart; however, the Retention Advisors will need to be bright, but not astute enough to research the company in-depth, otherwise they'll see through your attempts to camouflage the actual job duties.

If during a job screen for an open Retention Advisor position the recruiter notices the candidate asking far too many ethical questions, the recruiter should cut the interview short and ditch the candidate. As an example, consider a candidate who asks questions such as:

> "What is your philosophy on student retention? How do you prevent underprepared students from being retained unethically? What steps are taken to ensure your students are in programs that align with their career goals? How do you protect at-risk students from taking on substantial loan debt? How do you prepare students for loan repayment? What percentages of your first-time college students are retained, graduate successfully, and obtain full-time jobs in their intended career fields? What best practices do you follow? How much training do you and your Retention Department receive from outside academic professionals? Who accredits your school, and when was the last time the accreditor visited?"

Such questions are dangerous to your true mission as a sham enterprise. By the way, do you think the interviewer will be able to answer those questions? No way…and for a good reason. There are no legitimate answers to those questions, and you certainly don't want people knowing that. When a recruiter faces smart and perceptive candidates who leak through the screening process, the recruiter must avoid answering questions about ethics. Those candidates are future whistleblowers, pesky change agents, or won't last more than a few months in your business. They certainly won't adopt your brand's mission. Admissions Department candidates will typically be easier to filter since you'll be looking for the same demographic as the student population. The uneducated enroll the uneducated.

When looking for an Admissions Advisor candidate, the recruiter must ensure the job candidate is uneducated, lives paycheck to paycheck, thinks an office job is a launching point for a meaningful career and is susceptible to fear tactics common to call center environments.

Since your Admissions Department will have high employee turnover from staff who fail to meet unrealistic enrollment quotas, recruitment specialists should be invariably on the lookout for new and naïve college graduates, single mothers on the brink of financial ruin, ex-convicts who can't obtain work, and the sleaze who has no problem exploiting low-income borrowers for financial gain. In essence, recruiters should be selecting employees who are oblivious to the master plan, articulate and intelligent enough to communicate with low-income students, can integrate with the brand without questioning its ethics, and can be trained and controlled in a micromanaged environment.

Filter Job Candidates:

Since most of your departments will be micromanaged by tyrannical personalities, it'll be wise if your department leaders meet with each job candidate individually to assess naivety and loyalty - the two cornerstones to any unethical business operation. Because the open enrollment process is critical to your operation, enrollment directors should carefully filter candidates after the recruiter has screened for intelligence type and risk of potential whistle-blowing. It's appropriate to have top leaders choose their employees in order to implement the fear-based management model that aligns with their particular objectives. The Registrar Department staff won't need as much procreation of fear in comparison to the Retention Department; just as the Career Service Advisors won't need as much domineering as the Admissions Advisors.

The front-end departments with direct student contact are the divisions that will require ruthless leadership capable of intimidating staff to reach enrollment quotas, and capable of making workers behave like robots programmed to never question the company's mission. As an example, a recruiter may have selected four very qualified job candidates for an Admissions Advisor position, but only the Admissions Director should choose the candidate who can follow premade scripts without question.

You'll have to trust your directors to choose employees that'll work best in their particular divisions. After all, your chosen directors will have a flawed moral compass and a strong affinity for profit. They'll instinctively know which potential candidates have strong morals, and they'll immediately add those virtuous candidates to the do-no-hire list. Your directors won't be interested in dealing with new employees who are drawn to social activism, cultural awareness, and best practices in academia. Just one rogue employee with a moral compass can sink the entire ship, and you'll be paying your leadership far too much salary to jump ship or watch it sink.

Segregation is Key:

Most non-profit universities operate as cohesive entities with departments supporting each other for the better good of the student population. You must organize to be the opposite. You can have some cohesiveness amongst departments, as long as it's for two purposes: meeting regulations and earnings. Keep the departments separate and isolated most of the time and whenever possible. Information, procedures, and policies specific to one department should not be understood by another - this is critical for your operation.

As an example, if your Retention Advisors begin cautioning students about federal funding, you run the risk of vulnerable students withdrawing from the school because of poorly explained financial information. Immediately after starting the first class, students will be contacted by Retention Advisors weekly, sometimes daily. The Retention Advisors may form rapports with students and thus become inclined to help the impoverished simpletons avoid excessive tuition charges and additional debt, along with explaining the serious pitfalls of taking out additional funding without the means to repay. You don't want that to happen and end up losing access to your cash crop.

This is just one example of how a Retention Advisor with a strong moral compass can jeopardize the business - simply by trying to help a student avoid a serious student loan catastrophe. For this reason, the Retention and Admissions Advisors need to be completely segregated from the Financial Aid Department. Also, the Retention and Admissions Departments should be separated and isolated from one another; especially since a lot of conflicts will brew between these two departments regularly.

The Retention Advisors will essentially be dealing with extremely low caliber enrollees whom your Admissions Advisors force through the open enrollment gateway, and job performance will be measured by retaining a high percentage of those incoming buffoons. An Admissions Advisor will only work with a new enrollee for a few weeks, up to the point when the enrollee's attendance is generated and tuition is charged; whereas a Retention Advisor will be with that student for the length of time she's actively enrolled.

It's true, the Retention Advisors will see an extraordinarily low percentage of their assigned student cohort graduate, as most will fail, withdraw, or be dismissed within a few months of starting; but most of the Retention Advisors' day to day responsibilities will constitute servicing goofs who were not assessed for academic preparedness.

Retention Advisors will end up hating Admissions Advisors for the plethora of dimwits enrolled, and rightfully so. Despite what it seems, this conflict is healthy for your organization, as it drives a competitive environment were metric based goals are compared amongst these two fundamental sales departments. Instead of blaming you for the helter-skelter, the departments will blame each other. It's a wonderfully unscrupulous organization that will have you, the genius, at the helm.

Don't even try to mend the ill relationship between the Admissions and Retention Departments. It's an inherent feud in the business – like a sibling rivalry. If you feel inclined to establish peace between them, what will you do? Implement a protocol that involves an Admissions Advisor and Retention Advisor working side by side to ensure an enrollee is prepared for the first course? Such ideas are dangerous for a few reasons: For one, thinking outside the box and creating student-centered solutions is for the traditional university, not a for-profit college.

Secondly, the Admissions Advisor needs to get back to the job of enrolling more saps for the next session, not worry about the enrollee whom he just sold a fifty thousand dollar façade to.

Another reason to keep departments segregated is to protect suspicious policies. If every department knew the policies relevant to federal funding, tuition reimbursement, accreditation, and student grievance, then too many hands will be in the witch's pot. Every ingredient in the cauldron is necessary for an evil brew of lucrative greed, but the ingredients should rarely infuse.

Admissions Advisors should be kept in the dark about tuition reimbursement and student grievance policy; and the Financial Aid Advisors shouldn't know about the Admissions policies that make it possible for open enrollment to exist without academic assessment. Bottom line: the more ignorant the departments are of each others' policies, the better.

Chapter 5
Marketing the Myth

The cornerstone of your for-profit college is no doubt marketing. If you think it's education, you may want to close the book now and carefully consider your intentions. By now you should be aware of the reality that our business involves the exploitation of students eligible for federal funding and grants. You will not succeed if you can't market the business with this goal in mind, as devious as it sounds. If you try to focus your endeavors on education, it would be nearly impossible. You won't have the time or revenue to focus on academia as well as a business bent on making tremendous profit.

Don't shipwreck the business by putting money and effort toward the academic side of the operation; the marketing side takes priority. This can't be stressed enough. Allocate a higher percentage of your revenue to marketing instead of academic services. The most successful for-profit colleges do this to perfection and without shame.

The Dream and Cost:

From the first class to graduation, or more likely dismissal, you will be marketing the school to low-income students thirsty for a dream. A significant amount of revenue will need to be put into online advertisements, cold call efforts, and daytime and late-night commercials viewed by welfare recipients, depressed mothers, ex-inmates, and a host of other targets living in dilapidated communities across the country. For the purpose of this book, let's call these communities *Pell Communities*.

Some of the most prominent for-profit colleges have done extensive research to discover specific Pell Communities. Many of the Pell Communities are in southern states, as one can imagine. Whether broadcasted in a radio advertisement, on a coffee mug or T-shirt, or during a re-run of COPS, your Pell Community advertisements must convey that you are in the business of fulfilling dreams of success at an affordable price.

Once the suckers are caught and enrolled, the advertising will carry over into actual courses where students will write *dream essays* during course orientation – this dream-assignment technique will motivate new students to complete paperwork for enrollment and financial aid, and the Admissions and Retention Advisors can refer students back to their dream essays as a way to guilt and shame them during a withdraw request. Thus, marketing is an ongoing activity at your school and needs to be incorporated into assignments whenever possible.

Another effective marketing ploy is to encourage students to share news of their enrollment, course completions, and the Admission Advisors' contact information via social media, with neighbors, and even parole officers. Get the students to market to family and friends, who are also living in Pell Communities and thirsty for a dream come true. And if they don't have a dream to manipulate, utilize the power of shame and plant a fantasy in their desperate hearts.

Regarding the college's costs, market them as affordable; but relentlessly advertise opportunities for federal funding and grants. Establish a small scholarship option, but market it as a very big deal to first-generation students. Don't advertise the exact amount of the scholarship. The scholarship can be for veterans, student referrals, enrollees not eligible for the Pell Grant, or as a last resort to convince a schnook to enroll or remain enrolled. A scholarship between one and two thousand dollars should suffice. One thousand dollars is a lot of money for the average for-profit college student, so they'll consider it a significant reward despite the fact one course will cost roughly two thousand dollars.

They'll also have the chance to tell friends and family, "*I got a scholarship!*" It's a great marketing tactic: Their friends will think, "*If this bozo can get a scholarship, I surely can. He can't even spell his name correctly!*" Next thing you know, you're enrolling half of his family and the entire Pell Community. Besides the opportunity to receive federal funding and a scholarship, the best marketing tool is an actual purpose that can be believed and bought.

An Open Door Brand:

The first thing any business needs is a purpose that can be believed. It doesn't matter if the education you're selling helps anyone. What matters most is your target customer base falling for your brand's purpose and message like a blind person falling into an empty well. You must speak the prospective customers' language and learn about their fears. Offer not only what they want, but what they don't want, and speak to their circumstances.

Most of your potential students will be in need because they'll come from difficult backgrounds.: single mothers raising children on limited incomes, penniless young adults unable to get ahead of their debts and struggles, first-generation minority students with limited resources, persons with severe learning deficits unable to read or write past the grammar school level, the elderly in dire straits, disabled people who are desperately looking for support and help, the unemployed who are desperate for change and running short on savings, and the homeless. You'll have so many target customer populations that it'll be almost impossible to fail when branding your for-profit college.

The plethora of your customers will be uninformed, so your brand needs to focus more on dreams than actual education. Uninformed and ignorant people are more susceptible to dream marketing than forthright advertising. You might think potential customers will catch on to this dream approach and see right through the deception, but they won't. At times you might endure a moment of panic when a potential enrollee questions curricula, graduation rates, retention rates, tuition charges, fees, resources, pending lawsuits, and reviews; but later on I'll review ways to steer that prospective customer away from such trivialities. For now, let's get back to the topic of branding.

What does a successful for-profit college have that a traditional state or community college does not? The answer is *open enrollment*. Close your eyes and imagine people of all different ages, races, and backgrounds carrying heavy bags of money through the front door of your college, and saying, *"Thank you for allowing me the opportunity to go back to school! Thank you! Thank you! Thank you!"* Never discriminate against anyone who wishes to attend your college; every person is a potential victim.

You must welcome any human being that has a high school diploma or GED - the only requirement for attending your school. It doesn't matter who they are, where they're from, or how well prepared they are for college. What matters is they're alive, have proof of high school graduation, are eligible for federal funding, and can sign the enrollment agreement.

This is your brand: An open enrollment for-profit college that does not discriminate; offers low-income, first-generation, and non-traditional students a second chance; and does so affordably. You'll be saving the forgotten paupers of society from a traditional college system that brutally judges their intelligence, passion, value, and dignity. You'll be targeting vulnerable saps who've been turned away from over filled community colleges and state universities that told them *"We're sorry. You have not been chosen for admission to our distinguished school. We hope you the best in your future academic endeavors."* Your Admissions Department will enroll these heartbroken dreamers in droves.

So understand that your target market is huge; all you have to do is pick these ripe apples and gorge until you explode with bounteous profits. Of course, we know the community colleges and state universities offer a better education, have more resources, accommodate the disabled, have cheaper tuition, and enroll most students without bias; but our business is producing profits by enrolling any human being with access to federal funding. It's just business. If the customer has a heartbeat, we have a class seat.

Media Exposure:

If you follow the news and politics, you have undoubtedly noticed that the for-profit college industry is under a lot of scrutiny and attack by organizations advocating for low-income citizens, adult learners, minorities, active military, veterans, and a host of other groups you'll target for easy enrollment and access to funding. Liberal groups with well established social causes label the for-profit college industry in terms that are crass and despicable. Instead of defending your brand against defaming labels, embrace them!

Yes, embrace the most common labels used to denigrate your college. One of the most common labels is *predatory college*. The media and bleeding-heart organizations love to use the word *predatory* to label for-profit colleges, as they believe we deliberately prey on particular groups of dimwits who are susceptible to the dream approach and who can supply boatloads of financial aid. They're wrong - we are not preying on particular groups. We are preying on all groups! Receiving federal funding from particular groups is good, but receiving federal funding and grants from every citizen who has a high school diploma...even better.

If a giraffe could somehow obtain a high school diploma and receive federal student aid, we want to enroll the giraffe - it can't write, read, speak, or type on a computer, but neither can many of the goofs your Admissions Department will enroll. You must brand the school as open enrollment without discrimination, including any living thing that meets the basic requirements for enrollment. This sounds facetious, but it's not far off from reality.

For-profit colleges are also branded by the media as *diploma mills*. This is a label you shouldn't embrace; unless you're pushing students to graduate. It's strongly advised that you not set up the operation to push students through the program and to successful completion. We'll talk about this later, but for now, just accept that your graduation rate will be insanely low; and though you might think a low graduation rate will deter potential enrollees, it won't. You'll still have plenty of business with a graduation rate under 30%.

Without getting off track, just remember you are preying on a demographic in great supply, doesn't have the know-how or support to make an informed consumer decision, susceptible to manipulative and high-pressure sales tactics, responds favorably to the brand's *dream approach*, and reacts out of desperation. Being a *diploma mill* that graduates most students will only get you in hot-water with regulators and certain bureaucracies. It's in your financial best interest to graduate very few students. Silently accept the *predatory* label, but brand yourself as a white-knight who saves the forgotten paupers from a biased and cruel non-profit higher education system.

<u>Hypnotize Employees:</u>

Most of your employees should be on board with your brand. Drill it into their heads until you can see the dead stares and smiles. They should be walking around with fake smiles saying *"We do a great thing here. We do not discriminate. We openly enroll anyone who wishes to attend college. Every person has a right to attempt a college education."* As mentioned previously, if an employee has too strong of an ethical conscience and moral compass, fire him. If an employee begins questioning the abnormity of your brand, fire her also.

Tell them they were not the right fit for whichever position they held. An ethical employee could become a whistleblower if kept around long enough to see the big picture, and that's the last thing you need when your college is up, running, and profiting. Your employees need to accept and integrate into the brand or leave your organization. If a valued employee wants to leave, let her go – it's just not worth the risk keeping anyone around if there's suspicion they no longer believe your scheme.

For a paycheck, most employees are willing to accept and adopt an employer's brand; but you'll have the occasional outlier. To use an old and simple analogy consider the wild ocean: The sardine is eaten by the tuna, the tuna is eaten by the shark, and the shark is hunted and killed by the fisherman. Everyone has a role to play in the food chain. Some say it's sad, but others get the point and become powerful and rich. You're the fisherman in a sturdy for-profit college vessel. You don't discriminate against the fish - you catch and eat them, all of them. The lure is your brand, so bait every fish you can possibly attract with your charming dream message and customer service. Catch and eat. Release none. If a customer is lost off the hook, don't relent.

Have your Admissions and Retention Departments continually casting lines and nets to catch every foolish fish with has access to federal funding; and don't forget about the fish swimming together in Pell Communities.

Chapter 6:
Admissions: The Gateway to Destruction

At most non-profit colleges the enrollment process has an ethical goal. These traditional schools usually ensure the student being admitted is prepared and fit for the program and will not misuse federal loans nor go into considerable debt. The goal will be quite different at your for-profit college.

Your Admissions Department will have a simple purpose that'll involve enrolling as many people with a pulse as possible, getting them to sign the enrollment agreement, and having them establish active attendance. Without signing the enrollment agreement, the enrollee isn't responsible for tuition and cannot be held responsible for failure; and without establishing the first day of attendance, the enrollee doesn't become a student with federal funding to be exploited for your profit.

Again, the goal is simple: get the enrollee to sign the enrollment agreement, and then get her to establish attendance to start tuition charges. Once those two tasks are completed, the Admissions Advisor can move onto other vulnerable suckers who don't know how a for-profit college operates.

Though most non-profit colleges have strict admission standards, your enrollment process will be easily implemented as an open-enrollment institution. Remember, you'll have branded the school according to the open-enrollment model. Allow anyone with access to federal funding into the college.

Recall that your message from the start should be, *"Come one, come all. Let us help you achieve your dreams. We will not discriminate. We will accept you. We believe in you."* In effect, don't require any type of admission requirements that intimidate, expose, or repel potential customers. Trivial admission requirements such as essays, college preparedness and aptitude tests, interviews, GPA requirements, and long applications deter people who are undereducated and underprepared for the postsecondary level. The goal is to sell a dream, not an actual education. So, don't scare the customers off with academic entrance requirements.

By not considering sensible enrollment safeguards, your moral compass might be spinning out of control. Perhaps you're wondering how illiterate dullards will make it through your program to graduation, and ultimately to meaningful employment. You may, for a moment, feel that it's your obligation to caution or prepare illiterate customers for postsecondary challenges. That is not your job. If an enrollee can't write at the grade school level, enroll him anyway. The quicker he fails a course, the quicker you double your profit - possibly even triple your profit if he can't pass the course retake attempt. You can easily place the blame on the undereducated student by addressing the fact he's over eighteen years of age and signed the enrollment agreement. Don't worry about the consequences. The point is to keep business stakeholders content with short term gains; not ensuring students graduate on schedule or with a proper education.

Script:

The Admissions Advisor's script is key to ensuring students are enrolled legally yet kept from information that would deter them from starting immediately. The Admissions Advisor reads the script verbatim when speaking with a potential customer. You'll want to work with a legal team and industry consultants to design compelling scripts. If an Admissions Advisor veers off-script for any reason, fire him. When you fire him, ensure it's at a time when he'll have to walk past colleagues with head down and carrying a cardboard box filled with personal belongings.

The intent is to instill fear into advisors who are tempted to close a sale without sticking to the script. Train Admissions Advisors to stick to the script religiously. Develop your Admissions Department into a robotic sales force expert at selling dreams while obeying a pre-designed script.

Part of an Example Admissions Sales Script:

Introduction:

> *Hi, my name is [Insert Name], and I'm calling from [Insert School]. I was informed that you may be interested in attending college.*

If the prospective customer answers YES:

> *That is great to hear! Congratulations on your decision to complete your college degree. This must be very exciting for you. I'll be happy to walk you through the programs we offer and I'll address any questions you might have. Is now a good time to talk, or would you prefer I call back later today or tomorrow morning? I'll be your advisor for as long as you need. My goal is to help you make the right decision for your future. I'm here for you and want to be your personal cheerleader.*

If the prospective customer answers NO: (Discover pressure points)

> *I'm sorry to hear that this isn't a good time for you to attend college. When do you think will be a good time for you to finish your education and better your life? Life*

doesn't slow down, neither does time, so it may have to be now or you'll never go back to school. Many people put off college and never finish their degree, missing out on many opportunities. What is it that is keeping you from starting college courses? What is it you're struggling with in life right now? We all go through difficult times, but I want you to make the best decision for your future. I'm here to point you in the right direction. I want to listen to your personal story and get to know you. We're in the business of helping you achieve your dreams. You can start by enrolling today and working closely with me. What do you have to lose?

Once the advisor finds out what the person's struggles are – homelessness, joblessness, raising five children in a trailer park, gang life, depression, self-esteem, old age, etc. – then pressure points can be discovered and pressed to coerce the victim into a program that appears to resolve life's problems. The Admissions Advisor needs to sell the dream in order to instill a vision of a better life. The goal is to give the potential customer something to believe in: hope.

Advisors can arouse customer contemplation by asking questions like:

"Have you ever wanted to own a big home with a white picket fence, like in the movies? Wouldn't your children love to have a house like that, with a big yard and many

rooms?" or *"Flipping burgers isn't your destiny. Wouldn't you rather be wearing a nice suit every day to the office, with fresh coffee waiting, and your own parking spot? This can happen! First, you'll have to obtain a college degree, and we can help you get there. Don't you want to get ahead in life?"*

The Admission Advisor's script should offer suggestions and examples as mentioned, but much depends on how the prospective customer responds. Advisors should improvise questions based on responses. In essence, train your advisors to spot pressure points if prospective customers say *"No"* to the enrollment pitch.

First Goal:

The first goal of the Admissions Advisor is to get the prospective customer to sign the enrollment agreement. The agreement should be somewhat confusing. It shouldn't be short, clear, and comprehensible. Your Admission Advisors must be trained to rush potential customers through the enrollment process and into signing the agreement. It would benefit you to hire expert litigators who can develop the enrollment agreement and include ingenious clauses preventing students from suing the business.

The agreement should essentially place all responsibility on the student. Responsibilities such as starting classes with adequate funding, transferring credit from other institutions, being academically prepared, having the resources and time to attend online classes, understanding all the information about your programs, weighing financial pros and cons, and knowing all of the tuition costs and fees...are the responsibilities of the customer.

If a student blames you for exploiting her access to federal funding, point to the signed enrollment agreement and say, *"You're an adult. You signed the agreement. You owe us regardless of what we did or did not do. You knew what you were signing up for. Didn't you read the agreement before signing it?"* But don't answer so bluntly, because it's unprofessional and doesn't allow you to retain the customer for continued extortion. Candid responses are allowed if a customer threatens to sue you for malpractice; but until that point, keep communication professional and courteous.

Since your Admissions Department will be an expert sales force, you'll have to implement a micromanaged, metrics-based enrollment structure. The most prosperous for-profit colleges have large offices filled with gangs of Admissions Advisors competing to enroll as many defenseless suckers as possible. Digital counters are on the office walls showing which advisors and teams are ahead in the enrollment races, how many customers have been enrolled throughout the workday, and how close the department is at reaching the short term enrollment goals.

Even though it's illegal, according to federal law, to give bonuses as an incentive to enroll and retain students with Title IV funding, you can still offer non-monetary and indirect incentives such as trophies, recognitions, promotions, merit increase eligibility, and job security assurance. The fear of losing a job is powerful, and the greatest incentive is protection from that loss.

Admissions Advisors at for-profit colleges enroll the most defenseless and powerless people in our society out of fear of losing a nice paying office job. Many of your Admissions Advisors won't have a college degree, and they won't find a similar office job with comparable pay. It's enough comfort and anxiety to change an ethical person into a bloodthirsty salesman. A once decent person will become a sales expert with the acumen to convince a mentally handicapped victim into signing an enrollment agreement and take on astronomical student loan debt.

Consider offering your uneducated advisors free education at your for-profit college - offering this employee benefit creates another threat; if they don't meet their enrollment metrics, then they'll lose their free education as well. A more important reason for hiring uneducated Admissions Advisors is that you need employees who can understand, empathize, and speak the language of unintelligible prospective students. The best salesperson is someone who can directly relate to potential customers and has the disposition to exploit them. Since the Admissions Advisors will be reading a script edited by your legal team and paid consultants, the only real skill an advisor needs is the ability to convince a struggling single mother that your college is the answer to all of her problems.

Prepare the Admissions Advisors to use their own anecdotal stories or makeup narratives that'll convince prospective customers to sign the enrollment agreement. For example, an Admissions Advisor trying to close a sale can say to a doubtful prospect, "*I enrolled a woman who was working three jobs and raising two children. She finished our program quickly by accelerating her courses and was even eligible for the Pell Grant. She was also able to offset living expenses, as she was eligible for additional funding. The woman completed our program very fast and now has a college degree. Her life is 100% better, and her kids and family are proud of her. But most importantly, she's now a success and has pride in herself. This is a common story here at the college. A lot of people thank us for helping them achieve their goals and giving them a life they deserve.*" This is just one example, but can you imagine all the canny narratives the Admissions Advisors can use?

Degenerates with criminal records, transient homeless youth, destitute elderly, the severely disabled and bedridden, immigrants, mentally challenged, small-town indigents, the depressed and overmedicated…you have an endless supply of customers out there in this morose world. Your front-line employees must represent and effectively communicate the brand's message to these sad people. Revenue is dependent on it.

As mentioned earlier, enrollment metrics will be key to the success of your business. Call the metrics anything you want: Minimum Admissions Percentages or Minimum Admissions Goals, as an example. You'll need clear and defined metrics that Admissions Advisors and their teams can obtain and exceed to keep their jobs. To illustrate, perhaps you'll require advisors to enroll ten people per term, and also require that five to seven of those enrollees establish course attendance within the first week of starting. If an Admissions Advisor doesn't meet these goals on a consecutive term by term basis, then he can be placed on a performance improvement plan, which is essentially a warning that he won't have a job if he can't meet the benchmarks going forward.

When an advisor is placed on a performance improvement plan, imagine what he'll do to meet the metric goals for the next term: He'll veer off-script, make false promises, lie more than you expect and require, and do anything and everything to gain enrollments. This is great for you but bad for the employee. You'll gain the enrollments, but he'll have to be fired for being a liability. If this Admissions Advisor dramatically exceeds the enrollment benchmarks going forward, then you can keep him employed until enough complaints and escalations are made against him with regard to unscrupulous enrollment tactics. When Admissions Advisors go beyond your standard unethical operations, let them continue enrolling customers until a co-worker or student complains. Why terminate an effective Admissions Advisor so soon? Do nothing until he is exposed.

If this sounds like a boiler-room, call-center environment that creates conditions for high stress, competitiveness, backstabbing, stealing of leads, fudging of data, and high turnover…it is. The Admissions Office environment must be cutthroat. You can't have it any other way. If this makes you uncomfortable, don't worry too much about it; you'll hire a Vice President of Admissions who understands and controls this side of the racket. You should stay removed from this part of the operation - in case large lawsuits emerge, which they probably will if you're truly successful at this venture.

As you grow, the Admissions Department will generate a greater share of the company's revenue, so it'll be wise to hire multiple directors to oversee the Admissions Department. The more complex the web of Admissions, the easier it'll be to maintain an environment of obscurity, fear, and micromanagement.

One of the more critical times for your Admissions Department will be immediately before courses begin. You might think it'll be too risky to enroll customers just prior to courses starting, but keep in mind the goal isn't to care about your prospective students' odds of succeeding or their academic preparation. The goal is to get them to sign the enrollment agreement and establish attendance so you can receive taxpayer dollars, which can happen the day before, on, or after a course session begins.

Savvy for-profit colleges have made it an art to close sales soon after courses begin; that's when pressure can be put on a prospective customer. Think about it like this: You have a stressed out Admissions Advisor who needs to meet an unrealistic benchmark or else his job is in jeopardy, the courses have just started, and he receives a call from a poor sap who clicked on the school's online advertisement. In this situation, the advisor will do and say anything to enroll the ignoramus; like, *"Classes have started, but I can still get you in! You won't regret it. So many people have attempted to enroll, but missed the deadline; however, I can still get you in! Simply attempt the course and withdraw if you don't feel it's the right fit. This is a rare opportunity. It'll help you obtain a job, and you can use your new classmates and professor as references. Let me email you the enrollment agreement. Sign and return it within the next three hours."* There is nothing like the fear of losing a job, combined with benchmark deadlines, for increasing enrollments and profit.

Whether a last-minute enrollment is on the line, or a prospective customer is taking forever deciding on your college, the Admissions Advisors must think outside the box by suggesting more than one program. You'll need to have programs and concentrations that are named and advertised separately, but consist of the same courses.

As an example, if a person hesitates to enroll because you don't offer a Teacher Certification program, the Admissions Advisor can switch gears from attempting to sell the Business track and instead promote the Psychology program, which will mostly consist of business courses with a few basic Psychology classes thrown into the mix. The advisor can sell from the perspective that Psychology and Teaching are interrelated, and schools are showing increasing interest in teachers with a Psychology background since there is an epidemic of youth depression and mental illness in the public school systems. Of course, that's nonsensical gibberish, but the majority of people inquiring about your programs will assume the Admissions Advisors are trustworthy and knowledgeable about the job market.

Another opportunity to sell your useless degrees exists when a stooge calls the school inquiring about programs for becoming a Police Officer, Detective, Crime Scene Investigator, or Forensic Scientist. With an influx of law enforcement dramas on television, a lot of schmos fall into the trap of believing they can solve mysteries and homicide cases, simply because they're addicted to these shows. Your Admissions Advisors must capitalize on those naive beliefs, and sell your Criminal Justice program to these sheep. Six years later and tens of thousands of dollars in student loan debt, the customer will have a Bachelor of Science in Criminal Justice without any experience solving real criminal cases. You gain, and they lose; completely paid for with taxpayer dollars. Our business is ingenious - did I forget to mention that?

Second Goal:

After getting the prospective customer to sign the enrollment agreement and establish attendance, the second goal for the Admissions Advisor is to get the enrollee to submit her proof of high school graduation and ensure she is taking courses at an accelerated pace.

Without proof of high school graduation on file, federal student aid cannot be released. Remember, your objective is to be the custodian of the student's financial aid. To open up the flood gates of revenue, the student's proof of graduation must be on file before or soon after the start of the first course. The reason for the accelerated pace is simple: The more courses a student takes per term, the more money you acquire in the short-term. Two courses per term cost more than one course per term. It shouldn't matter to the Admissions Advisor whether the enrollee is prepared or able to take courses at a quick pace. Recognize here, the goal is profit; not ensuring a student is successful or graduates on time.

Critics will complain that you should first obtain a student's proof of high school graduation before accelerating her pace, to ensure she can handle the course load. Yet, do you care about the critics' concerns? If you do, you won't be profitable. If an Admissions Advisor enrolls a homeless guy who can't spell his name correctly as a result of brain trauma, the goal should still be to enroll him on an accelerated pace along with proof of high school graduation. The homeless guy won't complete your program, so get as much funding out of him in the first few terms by accelerating his pace.

Don't forget to establish a streamlined Re-entry Admissions Department focused on returning prior customers who have been withdrawn for attendance related reasons, by their own request, or for academic reasons such as probation or dismissal. The enrollment benchmarks for Re-entry Admissions Advisors don't have to be as strict or upheld since this type of returning customer wants to continue with your program. These returning students have already been brainwashed, sold on the brand, and have grown accustomed to the format of your university. In many cases, these victims have become addicted to receiving additional funding through Title IV and need the extra aid to buy food, pay rent, or support drug habits. The reason for their return doesn't matter. What's important is that they wish to return to the school, which for you simply means the returning of their Title IV funding to your revenue stream.

Make the re-entry process simple and streamlined: Don't require a re-admission essay, assessments, or evaluations to predetermine academic issues. You didn't have safeguards during the first enrollment, so why would you on re-admission? The Re-entry Admissions Department will be an important component of the overall operation, but a small one – as not too many customers will want to return to the sham. Also, don't pay Re-entry Admissions staff as much as your regular Admissions Advisors. The employees in your Re-entry Admissions Department should be experienced Admissions Advisors who've made you tons of profit in the front-end operation, but who are now burned out and need a break from the cutthroat sales environment.

Chapter 7
Retention: Keep and Plunder

As soon as you enroll those struggling single mothers and disabled veterans, you'll have to keep them enrolled for as long as they have funding to support your revenue stream. We call this *retention*. Think of retention as another form of admission. To illustrate, you have already admitted the customer into the program and have started to charge tuition and fees, but because there are so many factors threatening her to withdraw – such as her newfound realization that your program is subpar, expensive, and unable to meet her long term goals - you'll have to set up your operation in a way that retains her.

By this point in the venture, your Admissions Department should be well established, so the next step is setting up a strong Retention Department disguised as an academic advising or coaching service; yet is nonetheless a customer retention division. If you don't make student retention a priority, customers will withdraw or be withdrawn because of the Title IV policies that need to be enforced to receive federal funding.

Recall that you have to abide by certain federal policies to be eligible to receive and hold federal funding. Always keep this in mind, because if you violate any federal policies, then you put the business at risk of losing the qualifications necessary to receive federal money; and this can cause you to go out of business quickly. To be more specific, retention is the retaining of federal dollars for your revenue steam; not the retaining of students for academic success.

Your retention mantra must be, *"Attendance, attendance, attendance!"* You will not be able to retain customers if they don't attend courses. The dominant goal of your Retention Department is to get students to update their last day of attendance (LDA) at least every two weeks, so you can report them as active students who provide your revenue stream with lucrative federal monies. If an intelligible student realizes your program is a sham and thus decides to stop attending classes or stops submitting course work altogether, he'll eventually reach the attendance deadline and must be dismissed for reasons pertaining to accreditation and federal regulations.

So, how do you get the delinquent student to update course attendance? That's the question fueling every Retention Advisor. Your leadership team should stay up at night trying to solve the problem of deficient attendance. Retention Advisors need to be micromanaged to the point of absolute fear of losing their jobs if they can't get their student cohorts to update attendance. The mission is not about student success; it's all about student attendance. Updated attendance equates to increased and sustained profit.

Most everything that you put in place in terms of employees, policies, rewards, benefits, SOPs, structures...everything...is about the student starting the program and continually updating course attendance until she's withdrawn or dismissed. Understand clearly, the goal isn't graduation. The goal is getting the student far enough into the program to generate a profit for your business. If a student fails the first course, get her to update attendance for the next one. If a student doesn't have funding set up, get him to update his attendance regardless; you can always bill him outright.

Your Retention Advisors will be instrumental in keeping customers retained, and they'll be motivated to create ingenious ways of manipulating policies to keep their assigned student cohorts in attendance; their paychecks depend on it. The best Retention Advisors will be those employees who bombard students with emails, text messages, and phone calls to ensure they're updating attendance every day. When a Retention Advisor does his job appropriately, his students will be conditioned to update attendance without prompting. Students will update attendance simply to prevent the reminders.

You may be wondering, *"What about graduation rates? Isn't the point of retention to reach graduation?"* Recall that graduation is not the goal. Fool your students and employees, but don't fool yourself. Consider the caliber of individuals you'll be enrolling. Do you expect them to complete a college program taught by non-tenured adjunct professors with ethical standards and no loyalty to your brand? No way! And that's okay because the mission is to simply get the students to stay enrolled, day by day.

Do not measure Retention Advisors' performance using graduation metrics. Do not even inform employees of the actual graduation rates – the truth will do nothing but discourage your Retention Advisors. If you disclose the graduation rates, advisors will begin to think, *"What's the point in working for a college that isn't concerned about graduating students? Something seems off. I'm putting in all this work and none of my assigned students are graduating! On top of this madness, I'm being paid with the federal funding used to support my failing students. I wonder if I should report this to the state or government?"*

Such contemplation creates a breeding ground for whistleblowers, so keep graduation data out of the metrics reported to your general employees. Even if the school's graduation rates are miraculously increasing, profit is not dependent on graduation data. It pays more to have students repeat failed and incomplete courses, appeal probation and dismissal charges, and switch programs midway, than have students graduate with new and useful skills.

Don't forget to hire an intelligent and metrics focused director or vice president who can run the Retention Department carefully. It's in your best interest to hire a *yes-man* without a moral compass. This retention administrator must be able to speak academic lingo with legitimacy but operate the retention efforts as a non-academic manager. If the person, or persons, you put in charge of retention are bound to an ethical conscience, they may report your retention schemes to the Department of Education, the accrediting body, or the media.

Have the Retention Director sign a non-disclosure agreement before leading your retention efforts, and pay the person enough salary to stay monetarily dedicated for at least two or three years. Good candidates to lead your Retention Department are persons who have experience managing large call-centers heavily focused on sales metrics.

As with the Admissions Department, you'll need to incorporate metric based benchmarks into the retention side of your operation. It'll be important to assess Retention Advisors concerning the number of students willfully withdrawing and being automatically withdrawn for lack of attendance. Every Retention Advisor should have an excessive number of students to retain in an assigned cohort since it's not profitable to have them focusing on small groups of students. If the Retention Advisors become too involved with their students, they may develop genuine empathy and sympathy, which will increase the risk of purposefully directing students away from your sham.

The Retention Department's leadership team will need to set a baseline retention benchmark for each Retention Advisor: between 80% and 100% of each student cohort should be retained per term. If a Retention Advisor is unable to retain at least 80% of his student cohort per term, his job security should be threatened. Use carefully crafted performance evaluations as warnings to Retention Advisors who are unable to retain a benchmark percentage of students. Advisors will be so worried about their employment, and overwhelmed by the size of their student cohorts, they won't have the energy or ambition to help the students who are underprepared, struggling, and at-risk of failing every course in the program.

When it comes down to job security, even the most ethical Retention Advisors will compromise a moral compass for reaching an elusive benchmark related to a performance evaluation. Your greatest allies will be the rent, mortgage, or childcare bills that control your advisors. They'll retain hopeless students to simply meet their retention benchmarks and receive paychecks.

Similar to Admissions, you won't need to adequately train the Retention Department on current academic trends or best practices in higher education. The training for new employees should be kept in-house and conducted by a trainer whom you oversee.

There is absolutely no point in hiring an outside consultant who is an expert in the field of student success or sending new hires to learn from the most qualified student service professionals. Your new hires will quit within a few weeks if you expose them to competent professionals. I don't want you spending too much revenue on a constant hiring flux, so keep your employees unenlightened and incompetent. Outside influence from professional non-profit academic organizations can instill values and philosophies in new employees' minds that are counterintuitive to your mission.

You want Retention Advisors to blindly believe they're retaining students for a noble purpose, despite the likelihood most of their student cohorts will fail and absorb crippling student loan debt. As a reminder, do not let your new or current employees be trained, taught, or influenced by non-profit organizations that are experts in the area of student success and academic achievement.

I've mentioned the importance of student attendance multiple times and will continue to do so, but there is a second critical goal for your retention efforts that must be explained. When a student withdraws from your college, her federal funding must be sent back to the government. It's your responsibility to send it back; otherwise, you're at risk of being cut off from the lucrative streams of Title IV funding. The venture could fail quickly if this occurs. Though it's critical to keep students active at your college through conditioning of updated attendance, it's also critical to postpone students' date-of-determination (DOD). The DOD is another Title IV term - it simply refers to the date in which the student requested to withdraw from the school; so the job of your Retention Advisors will also involve getting students to postpone their DOD.

By postponing a student's DOD, you're holding onto their federal funding longer, which allows you to keep it in your revenue stream and available for expenses. You might be wondering, *"How can a Retention Advisor convince a student to postpone her withdraw?"* The answers are many, but they all center on tactful convincing and devious policies. Policies such as *leave of absence, course withdraw, course repeat, course extension, a period of non-enrollment*, and *incomplete* can be constructed and offered to students who request to withdraw. Retention Advisors are essentially experts in the use and manipulation of policies that impact the student's DOD.

Let's go through a few examples of retention:

Margaret is a student at your college. She informs her Retention Advisor that her husband was diagnosed with pancreatic cancer. Margaret requests to withdraw from her current course to care for her dying husband. She is distraught, stressed, and scared. Instead of honoring the withdraw request, the Retention Advisor is trained to re-commit Margaret to the program in order to meet the retention benchmark and secure his employment. To meet his retention goal, the Retention Advisor offers Margaret a *period of non-enrollment,* which is a devious policy that allows her to withdraw from the current course and return to the next term without officially withdrawing from the college. Of course it's in the best interest of Margaret to withdraw completely and return through the Re-entry Department, but we're not concerned about her best interests. Margaret's advisor convinces her to sign the *period of non-enrollment* policy agreement, frightening her into believing she might lose federal funding, additional stipends, and college credit if she withdraws completely. She takes the bait, signs the agreement, and pays the full cost of tuition for the course she's currently dropping. By signing an agreement to return in the next term, her date-of-determination is extended and the school gets to keep her federal funding.

Jeff is a disabled veteran who has been failing consecutive courses; thus, he generates a lot of revenue for your business. He comes to the realization that he's blowing through his military benefits, such as the G.I. Bill, as a result of not passing basic classes. Jeff's Retention Advisor has done a masterful job keeping him enrolled and updating course attendance. Jeff has been methodically conditioned to post a daily online assignment to keep his attendance fresh. Every term, Jeff's Retention Advisor convinces him that he needs to be persistent and eventually he'll see improvement. Jeff has severe PTSD coupled with a mild learning disability - he disclosed this to his Retention Advisor during the first term; however, the advisor's job is to re-commit Jeff to the program during and after each failed course. Because the school doesn't have a disability center or resources to support Jeff, the advisor directs him to an online writing center and third-party tutoring service, which won't help Jeff with his special needs. To postpone Jeff's date-of-determination, the advisor offers a *course extension*. Because of regulations, the extension can only be one week, which isn't enough time for Jeff to overcome his handicaps; yet, the advisor convinces Jeff that one week is enough time to make great strides in his academic journey. The Retention Advisor also appeals to Jeff's military training, reminding him that failure isn't an option and he'll jeopardize the mission of completing a college degree if he withdraws from the school. Jeff is successfully recommitted to the program, updates attendance by submitting an online assignment, and the Retention Advisor meets the retention benchmark.

Tierra is the average student at your school: A single mother of three children, working two jobs and living in a Pell Community. She is the first of her family to attend college. Unfortunately for Tierra, your Admissions Department convinced her that your school is the right fit for her needs; and fortunately for you, it's not. Tierra's Admissions Advisor did a stellar job convincing her to accelerate terms. As mentioned earlier, if a student is on an accelerated pace, you earn more profit expeditiously. The accelerated pace has been too stressful for Tierra, but her stipends, which she has become dependent on for living expenses, are only generated by the accelerated term credits. If she takes courses at a slower and more manageable pace, she will lose her additional funding. Burnt out, stressed, on academic warning, failing multiple courses, and racking up thousands of dollars in student loan debt, Tierra has come to a conclusion: The school is only interested in her access to the federal Pell Grant. Acting on her fresh epiphany, she requests to withdraw. However, being a savvy salesman, Tierra's Retention Advisor convinces her to stay enrolled by purposely failing and repeating courses until she appeals probation. The Retention Advisor tells Tierra that by purposely failing one course per session, she can continue receiving additional funding for living expenses, not have to withdraw from the college, and can inch toward graduation. After all, she can still pass the second course every session. Since she has invested so much time and money into the program, Tierra takes the bait and retakes courses purposely per her advisor's suggestion. Tierra's DOD is postponed until it's time to appeal her academic probation. By that point, she may have exhausted her federal loan limits; but that's not your concern, because she signed the enrollment agreement barring you from responsibility.

As you can see from these examples, retention is another form of admission. The Retention Advisors are simply recommitting students to extraneous programs. It's as if every student is restarting your program every two weeks, the time frame for which students must update attendance or be dismissed for regulatory reasons. The two-week attendance barrier will be your constant threat - it's a federal regulation you must adhere to in order to receive funding. Your Retention Department should be set up with teams of Retention Advisors who compete to reach the attendance deadlines. Daily phone calls, text messages, and emails should be sent to all students who have not submitted an assignment for eight days or more.

Until a student has updated her last day of attendance (LDA), she should be bombarded with truancy messages from your Retention Department. You can disguise and explain this type of harassment as great customer service, student coaching, or academic intervention. In fact, for-profit colleges have been recognized by state universities for their amazing customer service habits. Public colleges have even attempted to replicate the daily attention for-profit colleges give their ignorant student populations. Most people, even regulators, don't realize that the stellar attention given to for-profit college students is for one reason: the updating of attendance.

Since Retention Advisors have a lot of responsibility, it'll be important to help them manage each workday. If your retention operation is set up to include student cohorts, then advisors will have to prioritize the students scheduled for attendance dismissal.

An easy way to manage this priority is to send the teams a daily spreadsheet showing which students have not updated attendance (LDA) within the last ten to fourteen days. Retention Advisors can then start badgering students at day fourteen of non-attendance and work backward to day thirteen, twelve, eleven, and so on. Retention Managers should be checking on each Retention Advisor to ensure every student in every cohort is being contacted multiple times per day to prevent outdated attendance. The goal is to have each absent student submit an online assignment to update daily attendance, so you can generate a profit.

The second priority is to have your Retention Advisors contact students who've made official withdrawal requests and attempt to recommit those nitwits to the program. The recommitment process should be structured and strict. If recommitment fails, it'll be prudent to have advisors send their assigned at-risk students to a colleague. A separate advisor might use a different approach to convince students to stay enrolled or offer unconventional retention policies that the original advisor may not have remembered or was uncomfortable using. Retention Advisors must diligently take and keep detailed notes for each student interaction, especially re-commitment interactions. These meticulous notes will help managers identify advisors who are not committed to the university's exploitative mission and will help you develop more effective retention schemes. Also, the advisor's notes will convince pesky regulators that you're a professional and transparent business.

Another effective means of managing the Retention Department is through the use of student contact campaigns. Retention teams can compete to complete various campaigns by a deadline set by leadership. A campaign is a specific project that is focused on the retaining of a specific student population. For example, you can conduct a *Back to School* campaign, in which Retention Advisors are tasked with contacting students before a term's start date to ensure they update attendance to the upcoming term. Another important campaign would be the *Academic Appeal* campaign, which focuses on contacting all of the students in jeopardy of being dismissed for not submitting an appeal for academic probation or dismissal. Retention Advisors will race to contact as many probationary students as possible, to pressure them into submitting an academic appeal; that way, you can quickly approve the appeal and continue to legally abuse Title IV funds.

You can also have your Retention Department run a *Financial Aid Unpackaged* campaign, in which your advisors compete to have students submit missing Title IV documents. After all, if your students are slacking on the submission of funding related forms, you won't gain access to their funding. Campaigns are a great way to get your advisors to compete against one another while throwing your students into tremendous debt.

Moving on to next priorities: Recall that military students bring you enormous profits? As a reminder, active soldiers and veterans have access to unique funding that does not jeopardize the amount of Title IV funding your school is allowed to receive and hold. Because of their important contribution to your revenue stream, military students should be an essential priority to admission and retention. Market yourself as a *military-friendly school* and treat military students above and beyond the norm. In other words, do whatever you can to retain military students against their will.

Employ specialized Retention Advisors who focus primarily on the recommitment of military students. Consider hiring military veterans and reserves to your Retention Department, and assign them student cohorts consisting mostly of military students. Construct manipulative policies that cater to the life of military students, such as a *Military Leave of Absence*, which the Retention Advisors can use to convince deploying soldiers to remain enrolled via a short break. The goal is to keep a myriad of military funding in the revenue stream. Though you'll be promising better service to military students, you won't be treating them any differently than the regular student population. As with your civilian students, you'll be pressuring soldiers and veterans to continue with worthless programs that use up most of their eligible funding.

Your Retention Advisors will sometimes interact with spouses of soldiers and veterans. These military spouses will call the school requesting that their husband or wife be withdrawn for deployment-related reasons, such as being deployed overseas to an area without an internet connection. This is where the FERPA Law (Family Educational Rights and Privacy Act) can save you from having to withdraw the soldier, and thus lose their military funding. Unless the soldier submitted a FERPA form to the school, the Retention Advisor cannot speak with anyone other than the soldier. The soldier's spouse is forced to remain silent. This is a beautiful example of how a law meant to protect privacy is used to exploit.

In this particular situation, the Retention Advisor would simply tell the military spouse: *"I'm sorry. I understand that your husband is overseas in an area with no internet connection or means to communicate with the school, but I can't withdraw him from the program. I can't even speak with you unless your husband submits a FERPA form, which would allow the school to speak with you on his behalf. Legally, we can't speak with anyone other than the student without his permission."* The soldier's spouse will probably shout back in outrage, *"He was just called to deploy! Are you really going to charge him full tuition and let him receive a failing grade! I'm calling because I'm his wife, and he's in the middle of a foreign desert fighting for his country! What *you're doing is criminal!"* The Retention Advisor will have to simply, and politely, repeat the FERPA law.

Similarly, the FERPA law is used when a spouse, parent, therapist, social worker, caseworker, probation officer, or whomever calls the school and reports that a student is in the hospital, severely injured, in prison, dying, or deceased. The Retention Advisor can listen to the person relay the bad news about the student, but the advisor can't withdraw the student or stop tuition charges unless a FERPA form has been submitted. Thankfully, it's rare that students, and their loved ones, are aware of FERPA law.

As you can see, retention is just another form of admission. Critics of for-profit colleges are focused on the evils of the enrollment process, and rightfully so; but often forget about the retention aspect of the for-profit college business. This might be a result of retention being understudied and often not understood; which is great news for you. Colleges tend to define retention differently, and approach it from diverse philosophies – this ambiguity allows you to craft an especially effective scheme. It'll be in your best interest to give your Retention Department a misleading name such as *Student Advising, Academic Success, Student Success, or Student Coaching.*

Remember, the core of your business is misleading people into a useless degree program, so don't skimp on giving the Retention

Department an evasive name. Under the guise of life coaching, counseling, academic advising, and scholastic intervention, your Retention Advisors will be conditioned by fear and micromanagement to retain unprepared simpletons with access to Title IV and military funding.

Success is not determined by how many students graduate; it's determined by how many students you enroll and retain. If you can retain most students through the first half of the program, you're doing very well. If a student is retained beyond the halfway point, that's a bonus. Retention is fundamental to your business.

Chapter 8
Programs and Curricula

As you're aware by this point in the book, your for-profit college will exploit thousands of low-income borrowers with access to federal and military funding; however, you'll have to look and act like an accredited college with legal access to public funding. To act the part you'll need curricula and programs that appear legitimate and sell well. The most popular programs sold by successful for-profit colleges are *Business Administration, Information Technology, Criminal Justice,* and *Healthcare.* As stressed earlier, your college should be offering most, if not all, of these programs online.

Many for-profit colleges have a small brick-and-mortar campus located somewhere or will rent office space at a ground location, but make the majority of their revenue and profit online. It is highly recommended that you rent a ground campus location if you don't have one; but if you can't swing the expense, simply offer the academic programs online. You'll benefit from having a ground campus to give prospective students the impression you're an actual school. Online students will dream of visiting your ground campus someday for the graduation ceremony; but thankfully, most won't graduate, and the few who do graduate won't have the money to get to campus. Do you think your average student will be able to afford a flight or road trip? Never.

The beauty of offering programs online shows in the tuition charges. Tuition isn't any lower at online schools as it is at ground institutions. You can easily charge well over a thousand dollars for a five or six-week course; and since your Admissions and Retention Advisors will be pressuring students to accelerate terms, the average student will be paying between two and three thousand dollars every five or six weeks. Considering your programs run straight through the calendar year without long breaks, you'll be swimming in profit before you know it.

Offering programs online is more cost-effective and students can enroll from anywhere in the world, at any time. As an open enrollment school that doesn't discriminate, you'll be admitting suckers online all over the country. Have you heard of those seasonally depressed people in Alaska who haven't seen daylight for months and live on the edge of suicide? They are prime online customers for your business. Alaska must have multiple Pell Communities that you can enroll and retain.

The more degree programs you can offer, the better; but you'll have to be smart about the costs. A secret ingredient for program diversification is the general education course. Unlike certifications, college degrees require particular general education courses that are typically shared between programs. These fundamental courses are big money makers: *English, History, Humanities, Science, General Math, Algebra…* and the list continues. Whether the student is enrolled in a *Bachelor of Science in Business Administration* or a *Bachelor of Science in Information Technology*, she'll have to take *English 101, Algebra, History 101*, and *Science 101* regardless.

More than half of a student's program, regardless of the type of program, should consist of general education courses. It's paramount that you front-load general courses in every program. If a student takes a core content course too soon in the program, such as *Computer Science 101* in a *Bachelor of Science in Computer Systems* program, she may realize too soon that Computer Science is not her passion and you'll lose her enrollment along with the funding.

Bright students might request to take core content courses in the first or second term of their programs, but your Retention Advisors must be trained to encourage these students to keep taking general education courses. Train Retention Advisors to tell these canny students, *"The general education courses are safer to take in the first half of your program. If you decide to change programs later, general courses will easily transfer and you won't lose credit or be charged extra tuition. These courses may seem boring, but it's best to knock them out sooner than later. It's simply safer to do so."*

Another reason to front-load general education courses is to convince students that they're in the correct program, when they may not be. Admission Advisors will be intensely concerned about meeting enrollment benchmarks, so you'll have plenty of students pressured into programs that don't align with their needs. If students are taking general education courses in the first half of their programs, they won't realize they're in the wrong program until multiple terms have passed. By that time, you've made tens of thousands of dollars off their ignorance. Also, the general education courses consist of easier assignments and are taught by lenient adjunct professors who enjoy the extra pay; so your students will be under the impression they're doing great.

Think of general education courses as motivators that push your students deeper into programs that become more difficult and nearly impossible to finish. As mentioned previously, the goal isn't graduation; it's to retain students until the halfway point in the program. The Retention Advisor can easily convince his naive students to transfer to entirely new programs since they already paid for numerous general education courses. It's so easy to manipulate these poor suckers!

Regarding the structure of your degree programs, you can build them on a foundation of modules and terms. The best way to squeeze tons of profit from Title IV funding is to frame courses in modules and terms that span a few weeks in length. Financial aid disbursements become complicated and misunderstood within short modules, in comparison to long semesters. Customarily, one term consists of two modules; and Title IV funding is disbursed only by terms. So, to aptly maneuver the Title IV disbursement schedule, you can make course modules five or six weeks in length, which shortens terms to eleven weeks - instead of the traditional fifteen week-long semesters. Keep breaks between modules short, only a few days. According to Title IV funding laws, a student must update attendance in the second module of a term for you to obtain and keep 100% of her funding.

All of this may seem confusing, but just remember to construct your programs using short modules and terms, not semesters, to legally exploit students and have full access to their funding. Establishing shorter modules also allows your students to take accelerated terms, which puts more money in your pocket than a semester structure.

To make your programs look legitimate, hire curriculum designers to create the degree programs along with the assignments used for each course. Recall that your general education courses will be shared between programs, so have your in-house faculty work with curriculum consultants to formulate those shared gen eds. Specialized consultants can be a significant help when designing the core courses – it might seem like a waste of revenue to pay a specialist, since most of your students won't even make it to the core content courses or graduate; but remember, your college will be accredited and held accountable to provide a seemingly real education. Pay as much as you can to design decent curricula, and ensure the specialists also construct standard assignments for each online course. Your faculty members should simply follow the pre-designed curricula, send attendance reminders, and submit grades to an online portal.

Adjunct faculty members will make up roughly 95% of the Faculty Department; so keep adjuncts on short contracts, and try to hire a few professionals in the field. Don't skimp on their pay – try to pay adjuncts well. It's important to advertise as a college that employs professors with real-life experience in the subjects they teach. You'll experience adjunct professors who'll become frustrated and annoyed by the imbecility of your student populations, even in the upper-level courses, but that's not your problem. Remember, you've already factored into the business model that 75% of your student population won't graduate. Don't let professor grievances impact your core mission.

Adjunct instructors should report to a full-time faculty member who you've vetted and who understands the company's exploitative mission. That full-time faculty supervisor will be responsible for fielding professor complaints about student neglect, lack of training, and escalations; the supervisor will also be responsible for encouraging adjunct instructors to inflate grades in the general education courses and motivating students to update attendance. The adjunct professors whom you hire should be relatively clueless about your for-profit college scheme. Like the students, they should be under the impression you own a legitimate college. After all, you'll have regional accreditation.

Even though it's been brought up a lot, attendance needs to be mentioned yet again. The programs must be designed to make updating attendance easy and habitual for your students. The way to do this is through the slick development of mindless assignments. Discussion Boards are assignment submission platforms that many online for-profit colleges craftily utilize to trap student attendance and drive revenue. Typically, students will log into their online courses, and then enter a discussion forum where they're instructed to post responses to basic questions that are considered assignments.

By posting to a Discussion Board, students' online attendance is updated and federal funding begins flowing into your business. Considering how easy this is to implement, all of your courses, even high-level core content courses, should include Discussion Boards for every week of the term. If a student is on the verge of being withdrawn for not updating attendance by the deadline, the Retention Advisor will contact the student and have him submit an effortless post. The student's posting can even be gibberish, such as his name or the phrase, *"I'm not giving up. I'll submit the next assignment soon."* Any Discussion Board submission triggers student attendance, which is your bread and butter.

You can even have an app created to allow students to submit discussion forum responses from their smart-phones. Imagine the possibilities: A student calls the school and reports that she's now homeless because of a recent domestic dispute, and thus lost access to her computer. The Retention Advisor can spew drivel such as, *"I understand you need time away from school to find a secure living environment, but why drop out? Just log into your course's Discussion Board from your phone and post something. Post anything. That'll keep you enrolled and hopefully you'll pass the course."* You'll be wise to have the first assignment of each course be a Discussion Board posting, perhaps a mandatory class introduction; this forces all students to generate attendance quickly and easily at the start of each session.

Adaptive learning systems can also be used as assignments that generate attendance quickly and easily. Instead of having students conduct research and write lengthy papers, your programs can incorporate personalized learning software that self generates lessons throughout each course. Think of these assignments like online multiple-choice tests: Every time a student answers a question wrong, lessons are auto-generated and provided for the student to work through with additional testing at the end; as a result, students are constantly required to answer new questions for new lessons.

As a student works through the adaptive learning system, attendance is immediately generating - it's a highly effective means to manipulate student attendance and DOD. The alternative to this automatic scheme would be the traditional assignment expectations that involve completing a paper and uploading it. So many things can go wrong with the traditional upload strategy for course work: The student might not complete the paper, give up, forget to upload it, or won't know how to upload it. The uploading of documents, presentations, and spreadsheets makes updating attendance more difficult, so the more automated your assignments are, the better. In reality, the student learns more effectively when challenged to write, along with actual instruction and critiquing; but your goal isn't effective educating, it's getting the student to update online attendance. Never lose sight of the true mission.

Another benefit of the adaptive learning systems approach is that the results can carry over to courses that share similar content. An auto-generated assignment in a *Business Management* course can automatically transfer results to a *Marketing* course consisting of similar lessons. Students will be glad they won't have to repeat lessons, and this ensures a few of your students make it to graduation. It was mentioned earlier that graduation isn't a concern, but you still need to graduate a few of your students to appear legitimate – allowing students to repurpose and reuse course work will help with this great feat.

Using the same assignments in different courses and programs also saves you on consultancy costs. You'll have to tell the curricula designers that you want assignments and lessons shared between courses and programs. There will be a few students who catch on to this devious tactic, but only a few. If that occurs and customers question why they're not learning anything new and just repeating content, simply have Retention Advisors play dumb and tell them you'll look into the matter. Such complaints usually die with the passing of time.

Overall, the curricula for each program should consist of common general education courses and a few core content classes pre-designed by outside experts. You can offer Associate level programs, but Bachelor level degree tracks are more profitable. Offer both levels if possible. Concerning Master level programs, include a few and make them an extension of the Bachelor level equivalents. The difference between a Master and Bachelor program should simply be a few extra assignments and some research expectations, but don't go overboard with the research expectations. There are free online libraries that offer access to peer-reviewed articles and journals; so have your students utilize those free resources, and train your faculty members to be lenient with regard to students' Master level research.

At the Associate and Bachelor levels, don't require students to conduct real research. If research must be required for an undergraduate assignment because of regulator expectations, make the references and content readily available and packaged nicely within the online course. Even if you provide all the research necessary for an assignment, your dimwitted students will fail at alarming rates; which is okay. In the end, you'll still profit.

You might be wondering about faculty lectures. Since your college will be operating primarily online, keep class lectures limited to one or two hours per week. Students can log into your online campus when professors host live lectures at remote locations, or professors can prerecord video lectures and upload them to their online courses. Professors can also email the lecture recordings, or the links, to students. Don't require your students to attend lectures.

Remember, attendance is only generated by the submission of course work. As single mothers working multiple jobs, elderly experiencing hearing loss, and homeless people without an internet connection, your general student population will be too busy or unable to listen to live lectures held online. Your professors might feel bad about the lack of students watching their online lectures, but they're being paid regardless. However, you should still hold the professors accountable to provide weekly lectures that provide adequate content and teach to the premade assignments. It's still important to get a few of your students to graduation, and you need to appear like an accredited college.

As your business grows, pay attention to which programs are lacking enrollment and which are exploding in attendance. There will be times when you'll have to discontinue a program because it's not drawing the enrollment you need to sustain its costs. Program Chairs should be assigned to each program to monitor enrollment, faculty, content, and marketing. At normal universities, Program Chairs are held in high esteem with impressive academic qualifications.

Your Program Chairs need only to be capable of assessing the enrollment and retention metrics for their assigned programs. One of their primary roles will be to assist the Marketing Department in developing online popup ads that appeal to the program's target customer base. For example, the Program Chair for *Criminal Justice* should be up-to-date with current trends and topics in security, protection, and crime investigation, while working with your Director of Marketing to develop catchy advertisements that sucker in the most vulnerable crime investigator wannabes. Those advertisements can generate on popular conspiracy theory websites viewed by weirdoes who perfectly fit your customer base.

Chapter 9
Accreditation: Legal Extortion

Think of accreditation not only as a critical and professional endorsement for your business but also as a necessity for obtaining and holding federal funds. There are two types of accreditation available to colleges: regional and national. Strive to obtain regional accreditation. Don't worry; it won't be too difficult to obtain accreditation once you learn the politics involved. You might even be able to obtain accreditation indirectly.

Successful for-profit college entrepreneurs have bought failing and cheap accredited schools that were unable to stay afloat. By purchasing a regionally accredited college about to close down, you'll have instant accreditation and can wipe clean any ethical standards previously held by that institution. You can then turn that old accredited school into a profit-generating machine in no time with a few deficient programs and corrupt leadership.

If you decide to purchase a small accredited college, don't worry about the accreditor overseeing the school. If you violate any of the accreditor's ethical standards, ignore accreditor policies, or fail to report federally mandated data, you'll still be able to exploit low-income borrowers. The accreditor will not be concerned with your behavior as an institution of higher education; the accreditor is more concerned about your ability to grow and generate enough revenue to cover accreditation fees and dues. Consider payments to the accreditor as a business expense, or as profit sharing. It's just business – you have to pay your dues to the accreditor to be eligible to receive and hold Title IV funding.

If you're not in a position to purchase a failing accredited college, then you'll have to fill out the necessary paperwork to get started on the accreditation procedure, which you can find online. This will take a little time, but why not get started building your curricula and staff. You can even start enrolling students without solidifying accreditation, as long as they're signing enrollment agreements that disclose your school as non-accredited while you're in the process of obtaining accreditation. As previously mentioned, the enrollment agreement should protect you from all possible avenues to being sued.

Accreditation is essentially the gateway for federal funding. Without it, you won't have a lucrative and profitable business. It's commonly reported by industry critics that for-profit colleges receive 90% of their revenue from taxpayer dollars. This is accurate. We wish it could be 100%, but there has to be some limitation on our extortion of federal and military funds. Keep in mind that enrolling and retaining military students opens channels to non-federal funds that expand the 10% revenue gap not filled by Title IV funding. Remarkably, our government gave accreditors full power and discretion to award federal and military funding to for-profit colleges.

If you're concerned the government will hold accreditors accountable for decades of extortion, don't be. As long as you obtain regional accreditation and enroll enough low-income borrowers to compensate the accreditor, you won't lose your license to receive Title IV and military funding. There may be a time when the accreditor places your college on warning or probationary status, such as when you falsify graduation or career placement rates; but that'll be a gentle slap on the wrist. Even when you manipulate fiscal data that must be reported to the government, you'll be protected. The accreditor has your back. Think of your accreditor as a forgiving paramour.

Though the primary benefit of accreditation is the authorization to misuse taxpayer dollars, the other benefit, which is often overlooked, is protection. If enrollment numbers increase annually and you report decent quarterly retention rates, the accreditor will recognize your business as a profitable partner that can be relied upon for payments. If you make substantial money, then the accreditor won't want you to lose position in the market and it'll reject accreditation applications from potential competitors. Many wealthy egos desire to start a for-profit college, so you don't want those deep pocket tycoons attempting to steal your customers. If you become tight with an accreditor, paying dues on time and being a loyal compensator, the accreditor will make it difficult for potential competitors to take a piece of your customer base.

The more profitable you become, the better a friend the accreditor becomes, and a network of politicians and lobbyists will be open to you as a powerful resource. You've truly become filthy rich if you ever reach this point in the venture. The goal is to become so profitable with an accreditor's blessing that other devious entrepreneurs won't even consider stepping into your territory.

Once you acquire accreditation, you only have to apply for renewal every ten years or so. That's ten years of licensed extortion! Of course, you'll have to endure an occasional visit from the accreditor; but don't forget they're an ally. Always prepare staff for the accreditor's visit. You might assume their visitation will be spontaneous, but they'll give you notice of their expected arrival - this gives you plenty of time to train staff on how to behave and what to disclose to the accreditor. The accreditor simply wants to observe the basic operations, take notes for its files, and leave. They don't want to be at your office any more than you want them there.

Even though you and the accreditor understand the true mission of a for-profit college, it'll be important that you play the role of a legitimate school while they observe your Admissions, Retention, and Financial Aid Departments. Treat the accreditor like royalty, and prepare notes and reports for them in advance. Give them the material they need in case the Department of Education asks to see their visitation notes - though that will never happen, it's nice to be prepared and your accreditor will greatly appreciate it.

When the accreditor conducts a standard visitation or calls to address a complaint received from a student or government office, talk only about the positives of the college's operation. Mention your amazing customer service; show the notes and accurate records kept by the Admissions and Retention Departments; brag about your stellar *Net Promoter Score* showing customer recommendation; highlight your diligent retention practices and how staff contact at-risk students to ensure academic success; present the online resources available to your students; have the accreditor meet a few of your best Retention Advisors; and don't forget to remind the accreditor that the school's mission is to openly enroll people who've been discriminated by state and local colleges. If the accreditor must have contact with you, it'll appreciate if you're prepared and can make their job easier.

If you remain in this business long enough to reach the accreditation renewal period, then you'll have done extremely well and have built a sizable for-profit college. At this point, ten years have passed. For the renewal, it's recommended you hire an outside consultant that can train your staff to interact appropriately with the accreditor. Unlike the accreditor's regulatory visit, the renewal period will be more in-depth and the college will have to endure more scrutiny. The accreditor is still a friend of yours during renewal if you're producing enough revenue; but to protect its reputation, the accreditor will have to turn up the heat slightly. Pick staff members who have the acumen to sustain the accreditor's interviews, and have an expert consultant train those select staff to explain their job roles and responsibilities in a way that doesn't make you look like a scam.

When the accreditor arrives, the office environment should reflect less of a call-center atmosphere that preys on Pell Communities and more like a real academic institution. Essentially, you'll need to look like a real college for a short period of time. Once the accreditor completes its renewal procedures, then you can return the office environment to the metrics-focused, profit-generating monster that it is.

The accreditor will have official guidelines for obtaining and renewing accreditation. These may be titled *Criteria for Accreditation* or *Accreditation Requirements*. You, along with the leadership team, should become familiar with the guidelines, but don't panic because of the administrative wording in the guidelines. By the first look, it'll appear that you're violating half of the regulations – which you are, and the accreditor is aware. The purpose of becoming acquainted with these guidelines and regulations is to learn the lingo, so your leadership team can speak with the accreditor appropriately. The accreditor will believe everything you report - as long as you use the correct vocabulary.

As an example, one guideline may mention the *public good*. Of course, you are destroying the very fabric of the public good, but you won't blatantly disclose such truth. The guideline will stress that you shouldn't prioritize the business's financial interests over academic responsibilities. The entire business will be based on putting your financial interests above the betterment of your students; yet you'll tell the accreditor that your revenue is being invested back into the academic operations, which support the best interests of your diverse student population. You might worry the accreditor will call your bluff, since your financial statements will show the revenue isn't going toward academic support operations; but remember, the accreditor is your partner and not interested in losing your dues and fees. So, learn the lingo and play the accreditor's game.

Without accreditation you won't exist as a profitable enterprise, and you won't have the protection needed to keep competitors at bay. Accreditation is a legal license to steal. Once considered a professional accountability partner with the power to revoke a school's access to federal funding, an accreditor is just an extension of your insidious operation, as long as you're able to compensate. If you want to become filthy rich, obtain accreditation and follow the principles in this book. It's not about providing a quality education, but making a profit.

Chapter 10:
Compliance: The Fishing Guide

Accreditation is a must-have, but so is staying in compliance with federal laws. Don't even consider starting a for-profit college business without compliance officers in place to protect and defend your stratagem. Great legal counselors will ensure you're going about your business in agreement with federal and state laws. One of the primary reasons you'll become so incredibly rich is the business's ability to stay out of legal trouble. It's paramount that you manipulate federal and state funding regulations with supreme acumen.

As you know by now, accreditors are as corrupt as for-profit colleges, but it's still important to have lawyers who can protect your business from potential legal onslaughts from defrauded students, whistleblowers, and civic leaders. Accreditation alone isn't full protection, but accreditation with a strong compliance team creates dynamic security.

Acknowledge all the ways for-profit colleges have been sued over the last few decades: falsifying career placement rates, lying to prospective students during the enrollment process, incentivizing enrollment and retention, ignoring state and federal rules, soliciting Title IV borrowers through lead purchasing, purposely reporting inaccurate data to the Security Exchange Commission, retaliating against whistleblowers, and the list goes on and on. Such legal problems are enough to scare off any savvy entrepreneur wishing to make a living by exploiting desperate, poor, and disabled Title IV borrowers.

Depending on the highest political authorities of the time, it can be easy or difficult for the for-profit college industry to do its damage on society. But even when political winds are working against for-profit college chicanery, strong legal counselors and compliance teams can help catch and clean as many Title IV borrowers as your greedy heart desires. There might never have been a better time in history for you to go fishing for those vulnerable paupers who believe an online for-profit college is worth the investment and lifelong debt. Think of your compliance team as your fishing guide, and accreditation as the charter boat.

Staying up-to-date on federal and state rules and regulations takes a lot of time and effort - this is what your compliance team is paid for. Since the majority of the operation is directly, and indirectly, involved in fraudulent activity, your compliance team will need to have a say in almost everything you do.

Let's say the Admission's Director is considering a change to the call script, which is read to all prospective customers. In this example, he wants to change one measly sentence in the script that refers to the transferring of prior college credits. You should terminate his employment immediately if he makes the change without consulting your compliance team. One such minuscule change in the Admissions Advisor's call script can be a weak spot in your armor and can result in a lawsuit too big to survive. Admissions Department call-script revisions, retention protocol, mass attendance notifications, changes to any retention policies, the reporting of metrics to the government, termination of a problem employee or whistle-blower...these are some of the things that need to be reviewed and approved by your compliance team before taking action.

It's critical that you play by the federal and state rules, even with the accreditor as your paramour. Students and ex-employees have sued for-profit colleges from various angels; such as the False Claims Act, human rights violations, consumer fraud suits, and via the Security and Exchange Commission.

As you grow powerfully rich, it'll be wise to start diversifying your compliance team to focus on specific areas of the operation. Hire an in-house lawyer to focus entirely on Title IV funding regulations, have another legal counselor keep track of state regulations since you'll have online students in various states, and don't forget compliance officers who specialize in military funding, the Federal Trade Commission, and the Equal Employment Opportunity Commission (EEOC).

Since your Admissions and Retention Departments will have high employee turnover, you'll certainly have at least some workers who report discrimination to EEOC and file a lawsuit. Your Human Resources Department and EEOC compliance officer must work together to find legitimate and effective ways to terminate employees, ensure that departments are diversified to protect you from discrimination lawsuits and keep employees trained on current compliance procedures involving LDA and DOD. Even in states where termination is at the will of the employer, you should protect yourself from EEOC lawsuits and present the business as nondiscriminatory. One of the easiest ways to ensure this is to hire mostly minorities for the enrollment operations. It's a win-win situation – with minorities enrolling your students, you'll have an employee base that understands your customers and you'll save the business from pesky discrimination charges.

The compliance team will also be beneficial during student escalations that demand tuition forgiveness. At first thought, tuition forgiveness may sound like a great idea: If you enroll thousands of students through a call-center Admissions Department, who cares if you have to refund tuition to a few complainants? Well, even though you can quickly offset a tuition refund, you won't want to start a trend or expose the college to a discrimination lawsuit. For instance, if a student asks for tuition forgiveness because her Admissions Advisor sold her the *Accounting* program, even though she initially asked to be enrolled in the *Marketing* program, this might seem like a legitimate case for a tuition refund. But you'll probably be enrolling hundreds, if not thousands, of people into the wrong programs; and the Retention Department will be recommitting students into programs that certainly don't align with their career goals. If you allow tuition forgiveness for one student, you'll have to allow it for all students; and if the student is a minority, then you'll have another issue in the making.

Bottom line: Your compliance team needs to be involved in every request for tuition forgiveness. As soon as a student requests a refund because of something the college did or didn't do, have your Retention Director contact the compliance team to research the situation and provide a justifiable response to the student. Rarely should tuition forgiveness be granted. Only in cases where a student involves a lawyer, threatens to involve a lawyer, or persists to the point of using way too much of the business's time and resources, should you consider granting tuition forgiveness. Thankfully, the majority of your student population will be too vulnerable, clueless, uneducated, and scared to persist or threaten a lawsuit.

Even if you can't afford a sizable compliance team when starting the college, simply adding one lawyer to your full-time staff will be a big benefit. If you are starting out small, then retain outside counsel; but as you grow, having a full-time lawyer on the payroll will save you lots of money. Outside counsel can cost thousands of dollars per hour when sizable lawsuits threaten your business. In-house legal counsel can represent you at discrimination hearings, EEOC and state fact-finding conferences, and can handle the small obstacles while passing the bigger lawsuits to outside counsel.

You might be wondering, *"How do I find a lawyer who's this corrupt? Who would put their reputation on the line by defending a for-profit college? Isn't that career suicide?"* That's a legitimate question, but rest assured that there are plenty of lawyers who will jump at the opportunity to defend a for-profit college. Many lawyers are in it for the money, just like you; and it's no secret that for-profit colleges bring in lots of revenue from taxpayer dollars. Taxes aren't going away, and taxes rarely decrease, which means a business built on taxpayer-funded loans and grants will be lucrative for a long time. Many lawyers recognize this fact and will gladly take a job protecting and defending a shady business like yours. If the lawyer does a great job keeping you afloat, he knows he'll be rewarded well.

Having a compliance team, an own in-house lawyer, and outside counsel can seem like a waste of revenue. It's expensive to have and keep counsel; but from a business perspective, it's the smartest thing to do if you plan on starting a for-profit college. As mentioned, you'll have many critics and political winds can change at any time, making you highly susceptible to lawsuits.

Bleeding-hearts, patriots, and progressive liberals don't want you succeeding as a for-profit college entrepreneur. These adversaries know what you're all about – profiteering off low-income borrowers eligible for Title IV and military funding.

Some of your critics will be relentless in attempts to put you out of business. They may often bring lawsuits from various angles, using whistle-blowers and angry students as catalysts. Not having protection against opponents is a recipe for disaster. You can be successful in the short-term without skilled counsel, but in the long-term you're looking at prison. Keep a healthy, vibrant, stunningly corrupt for-profit college by keeping reputable legal counsel and a competent compliance team.

Chapter 11
Ignorance Pays

Now let's change gears and speak to the philosophy behind the operation and student costs. There is a correlation between homeownership and for-profit education that would be wise to study. Why do you think so many people continue to buy houses when homeownership has shown to be a fairly weak investment? Not only is it a weak investment, but way too many existing homeowners hate the debt burden caused by their home. Consumers who haven't been taught to keep a monthly budget continue to apply for mortgages and buy homes they'll never be able to pay off. The reason for this common homeownership tragedy will also be the driving force for your success. That reason is none-other than *customer ignorance*.

Ignorance is a moneymaker, and when starting a for-profit college you must ride the wave of public ignorance to financial glory. Pay careful attention to the homeownership trap; it can be an effective teacher throughout the building and sustaining of your for-profit college business. Like the debt-laden college students who've blindly trusted Admissions Advisors, many new homeowners have ignorantly followed the advice of realtors and proceeded in the footsteps of relatives and friends who are drowning in mortgage debt.

You probably know a few people who are looking to buy a home. They're getting all kinds of advice from ignorant and well-intentioned friends and family; believing realtors who have branded themselves as expert real-estate market professionals. After much convincing from a savvy realtor, your friends probably applied for a mortgage and was happy to get it with a 5% to 10% down payment; next, they probably calculated the cost of the 30 year mortgage, with interest rates and taxes included, and felt the adrenaline and endorphins intensify as they realized this is one of the most important financial decisions of their lives. These sheep desire to prove to their family, friends, and more importantly themselves, that they've reached an important milestone in adulthood. When the home sale completes and the documents are signed, the realtor and mortgage broker get their share of the pie. Soon after that, grim reality begins to set in, slowly but surely.

Homebuyers typically look at the tip of the home-costs iceberg and believe it's the entire shebang. The tip of the iceberg is the down payment and monthly mortgage, but below the frigid waters are the expenses that people are too ignorant to discover and examine. There are tons of costs the average home buyer doesn't expect, nor budget for. Let's not get too far off track and discuss amortization, utility costs, insurance, property taxes, upkeep, closing and selling costs, etc....just recognize there's a lot to the homeownership iceberg. It's massive, and most of it is unseen. Realtors will rarely sit down with the homebuyer and examine the short term and long term costs and risks. The bottom line: You can benefit by studying the ignorance of most home buyers, examine the phenomenon of mortgage debt, and apply similar realtor tactics to your enrollment and retention operations.

As it wouldn't benefit a realtor to reveal the entire home expense iceberg, it won't benefit your for-profit college to disclose all the costs and risks associated with enrollment. If you are completely honest with new and continuing students regarding the costs and risks associated with enrollment, no one will attend or continue with your college. Don't be ethical at a time like this – if you are, you'll fail. Your customers must be oblivious to the short term and long term costs involved. They are ignorant to begin with, so don't enlighten them to the reality. You must let students discover the entire iceberg on their own. After all, you'll be protected by the enrollment agreement, which absolves you of any responsibility to consider the students' best interests before profit.

When students fall into massive student loan debt, that's on them, not on you. They're adults who can examine the massive iceberg of student loan debt on their own before enrolling at your school. You're not a financial service, so keep costs and risks out of the communication channel with prospective students. This cannot be stressed enough. If students wish to stare at the tip of the iceberg and not consider what's below the water, that's unfortunate for them and their families. You sold them the dream of a better life, but you're not responsible if they ignorantly believe the dream to their detriment.

This lesson may seem harsh, but it's important to address any ethical concerns you might have because this isn't the type of business that thrives on morals. Think revenue, think profit, think of students as customers who bring you both. It is ignorance of the costs that will make your revenue stream become a raging class-five river. It'll be critical to train your staff to discuss only the tip of the iceberg, and simply mention other possible costs when necessary. Any costs mentioned or included in the enrollment agreement should be limited to what the Department of Education and accreditor require. Let's now talk about some of the costs your students should and shouldn't understand, and how to keep those costs relatively unknown.

There's a difference between lying and simply being vague. If you withhold information, or misconstrue it and make the information appear confusing, then you're not to blame. As long as you have the total costs and risks buried in the enrollment agreement, or somewhere on your online campus - such as a student handbook or student resources page - the Admissions and Retention Departments don't have to clearly communicate that information.

If a student ever asks, *"How much is this course costing me"*, you can train staff to play dumb and refer the handbook, course catalog, or wherever you hid that figure. You can also set up the operation so students are sent to Financial Aid Advisors or team leaders trained to respond in your best interests - in other words, in a way that doesn't disclose the true costs. If an annoying student persists to question, then tell her the actual costs. You'll lose a percentage of students who catch on to your debacle. It won't be many, but you'll need to account for that loss. You'll make up the loss with the other 99% of your customer base.

Incoming students will have to be told the total costs of the programs in which they are enrolling, but they don't need to know the cost per credit hour. Many of them won't be smart enough to calculate the cost of a class using credit hours, so they'll rarely ask how much money a failed or dropped course will cost in the long term. Most students won't even inquire about tuition for course repeats; they'll ignorantly assume the loans cover failed courses and retakes. As mentioned previously, you will profit greatly from these failures.

Always remember the demographics of your customer base: most of them are destined to fail. Do you think a single parent holding down two jobs and raising three children will have the time and energy to fight fraudulent tuition charges? That parent will fail the same course four times, and you'll earn the full tuition payment for every attempt. Even if that parent questions the real costs involved in retaking courses, she'll lose steam as your staff passes her from department to department.

This is a good time to remind you that failed courses are a profit boost. As mentioned, most students won't question the cost of a failed course. Your operation will be so efficient that students won't have to reschedule failed courses - your staff will automatically process the rescheduling, which means students are less likely to question the costs and risks associated with repeated classes. Students, for the most part, are trusting individuals; especially when attending a college that sold them a false dream. The customers won't consider that costs are being withheld purposefully. Most students won't even know they're enrolled in a for-profit college. They'll think you're *for-student*, not *for-profit*. Ignorance is bliss.

Chapter 12
Customer Service: Reselling the Dream

Though you'll be cutting costs by averting revenue from academic services, customer service cannot be neglected; it will always be an important cornerstone in the for-profit college world. One can argue that your entire business could slowly crash without exceptional customer service. Keep in mind, you'll need to disguise it as an academic resource, but it is not.

Your students won't realize the ominous guise, but stakeholders will praise you for it. Your Admissions and Retention Departments will be customer service empires, first and foremost, and most of your employee training will center on essential customer service principles. Never forget that customers will enroll not for programs with stellar academic, remedial, and scholarly services, but because Admissions Advisors made them feel special and Retention Advisors continued to sell the dream. You won't even need to cover up that customer service is a disingenuous tool cloaked as an academic resource.

Do you think half of the suckers signing the enrollment agreement will be concerned about the quality of your college? Definitely not. These stooges want to know that someone, anyone, believes in them. Skilled customer service professionals provide this deceit.

Who better to act as a phony cheerleader than your Admissions and Retention Advisors, who are under intense pressure to meet performance benchmarks?

It's not like your for-profit college will manufacture a useful commodity that needs installation, maintenance, or troubleshooting. It's a fraudulent service sold to saps who think it'll pay off in two to four years. That's the beauty of owning a for-profit college business - the customer won't know it was a sham until years after his Admissions Advisor sold him a bogus fantasy using exceptional customer service skills. Rarely will a student catch on and complain about the ineffectiveness of your program. Once they've been withdrawn, dismissed or graduated, regular students will be too embarrassed to raise a fuss.

If disgruntled students post bad reviews online about your school, it's not like the target customer base will discover and read those hostile reviews - many of them can't even read after a few terms, and many others seldom have access to the internet; plus, they'll most likely be too busy struggling with the daily demands of a low-income lifestyle to fuss. Don't for a second believe you have an obligation to continue providing customer service to failures who are no longer taking courses or providing you revenue. You don't. By spending two minutes listening to a student complain about her massive federal loan debt incurred at your college, you'll be taking time away from enrolling and retaining other fools.

But while these victims are actively enrolled as your students, your customer service needs to be five-star quality. Student retention involves fantastic response time and attention. Traditional non-profit schools are starting to examine for-profit colleges for their impeccable customer service procedures. Community colleges, state universities, and private non-profit colleges allocate resources to focus on academic needs instead of customer service. They don't understand why for-profit colleges receive amazing customer service reviews - but that's their problem.

Remember, traditional schools are not in the game of getting filthy rich, so they'll never have customer service better than what you'll provide. Non-profit institutions are actually interested in graduating students with well-developed skills that can be used in the marketplace; they believe this philosophy helps the school's reputation and enrollment in the long term. That's not your business. Never trade your customer service for actual academic service; if you do, you're at risk of tanking the business.

To implement amazing customer service you don't even have to train staff thoroughly. The more your staff knows about accreditation policies, student success resources, best practices, and even your college's own policies, the worse off you'll be. Too much information shared is too much risk. All of your departments must practice high-quality customer service, but they shouldn't know what happens in other departments. For example, if a student contacts her Retention Advisor to complain about sketchy tuition charges, the advisor shouldn't attempt to address the student's concern; instead, that advisor should pretend to advocate, and then pass the student along to the Student Accounts Department.

Customer service is simple. Don't make it complicated. It's nothing more than replying quickly to a student, listening without supplying complete and accurate information, behaving politely and respectfully, and empathizing. I know what you're probably thinking, *"How can I empathize with a broke guy who has a severe learning handicap and lives in a trailer park home?"* You must train staff to pretend to care. If need be, hire an outside consultant to train your staff to deaden their senses to the students' dribble and respond appropriately. *"I understand. I'm sorry to hear that,"* or *"I'm listening. I can see you're upset. I'm here to help you,"* are great phrases your staff can use in any type of escalated situation. It'll be uncommon for your staff to speak with students who recognize this trickery. Don't forget, you'll have sold them on the dream of a better life, so they're already sensitive to whatever you say.

Great customer service is simply buttering them up when they need the reminder. You'll be surprised how easy it is to resolve a student complaint such as, *"My Admissions Advisor lied to me! He told me this $50,000 Criminal Justice program is needed to* *become a police officer. I have three courses left in the program and just found out I wasted my time and funding! I'm going to notify the Department of Education and Better Business Bureau. I'm thinking of suing."* In case you're wondering, the approach would be to connect the student with the Retention Advisor, who already established a rapport. The Retention Advisor will listen intently, repeat the phrases mentioned, and will improvise with some nonsense about how completing the program can result in a quicker promotion in the police department.

In the previous example, the Retention Advisor did not only resell the dream of a better life, but created a new dream. That's excellent customer service. The student felt defeated because of the great loss of time and money. The Retention Advisor did the correct thing by creating a more attractive dream and implanting a fresh fantasy into the student's mind. Great customer service at a for-profit college involves reselling the dream of a better life; and if need be, creating alternative dreams to keep the student recommitted.

Do whatever is necessary to sell and resell the dream of a better life. Think of your customer service as dream support. If it wasn't borderline absurd, you can label your Retention Advisors something like *Dream Advisors* or *Dream Coaches*. Considering the customer demographic, if you call the enrollment and retention staff by such frivolous titles, you would probably exceed enrollment and retention benchmarks every quarter. Though it's an interesting idea, don't be tempted to change titles; keep the industry titles already in place. As regulations ease up and the political winds favor the for-profit college industry, then we can get crazy and develop *Dream Departments* and *dream assignments* that reinforce students' fantasies of success. Even the accreditor will be okay with those frivolous changes when the time comes. After all, the accreditor will favorably report the results of an effective dream based approach through methods such as *Net Promoter Scores*, to show the Department of Education how well you're doing as a university. Don't forget, the more profit you make, the more inclined the accreditor is to protect the college.

Customer service is so effective at for-profit colleges that it creates a unique population of students who hate the school but stay enrolled regardless. For example, many of your students will be extremely agitated with the college's Financial Aid Department; but using savvy customer service skills, the Financial Aid Advisors, with the support of Retention Advisors, can apologize for delayed stipend allotments and remind students about the amount of time and money they spent on the program. Speaking always so gently, patiently, and appearing empathetic, advisors can turn a ferociously upset student into a quiet advocate of the university. One minute the student will be threatening to sue you for stealing her Title IV funding; and after encountering your customer service magic, she'll become your biggest proponent a minute later. After her experience with your customer service, she may even purchase a university t-shirt or bumper sticker, which she'll show off in her Pell Community. It's basic psychology: At the end of the day, the customer wants to be heard, accepted, respected, and cherished.

Not to say any of this is easy. Customer service at a for-profit college can be incredibly taxing on your staff. Think of the caliber of students the advisors will be contacting every workday. It's draining on a Retention Advisor when a student calls him terrible names because the student didn't receive additional funding to pay a bail bond, failed eight consecutive courses, or had a late assignment denied despite being arrested the day before the due date. Because your customer service will be first-rate quality, the advisors will be mistaken as counselors who care and the students will try to make the most of those relationships.

The student's university experience is created from the interaction with her advisors, primarily the Retention Advisors; so advisors must be patient, have a sense of humor, have amazing persuasion skills, and know how to prioritize attendance campaigns. As a critical reminder, everything, including customer service, is about the updating of students' attendance. Every customer interaction, even the heated escalations that involve the threat of lawsuits, should incorporate the goal of updating student attendance.

In summary, every department needs to interact with students politely, persuasively, and patiently. You can't skimp on excellent customer service. Without it, you don't have anything to offer. What would you offer otherwise: Legitimate academic services, quality content in your classes, student loan safeguards, and full disclosures about tuition and fees? If you still have a solid moral compass at this point in the book, you should reconsider your endeavor to start a for-profit college. Make no mistake - the goal is to profit from the ignorance of the vast pool of low-income borrowers who have access to bountiful funding. Excellent customer service is the net that'll catch these oblivious fish.

Chapter 13
Support

If you have all the gusto on the planet and are ready to build a for-profit college worthy of bankrupting the federal government, you'll still need sufficient support to start and maintain the enterprise. We've already discussed the support of accreditors and savvy lawyers, but other support is needed.

If your business gains significant growth, it'll be a sizable target for consumer rights activists, states attorneys, whistleblowers, and a slew of other entities desiring to protect the public good. The only way you'll grow your business is by exploiting more and more low-income borrowers, along with the taxpayers who fund them; and the more taxpayers you exploit, the more protection you'll need.

Going it alone in this industry would not be wise, so it'll be in your best interest to join a private college trade association that represents for-profit college interests. There are a few large ones in existence, and you can easily find them by conducting an internet search. These affiliate organizations are wonderful resources that can set you up with likeminded scam artists and may even introduce you to government lobbyists who fight to maintain your access to Title IV funding.

Certain political parties, not interested in the growth of your business, will often propose legislation that'll make it difficult to extract and profit from federal funding. You'll need fighters in the political arena who can protect your license to exploit low-income borrowers for decades to come. These well-paid lobbyists will fight to the death for the survival of your enterprise.

Associate businesses can also offer a solid support network. What types of businesses are dependent on the success of for-profit colleges? Many: Private student loan companies, businesses that provide materials and resources to boiler-room call centers, hedge funds and brokers, software companies that design programs to track and analyze enrollment and retention metrics, insurance companies, and debt collectors to name a few. Also, other for-profit colleges want you to succeed, as long as you're not a serious competitor. For-profit colleges usually support one another by accepting transfer credits.

Many traditional universities won't accept transfer credits from for-profit schools, but your partners in crime will come to the rescue. As a result, many of the students who enroll at your college will eventually be customers at another for-profit school after they've been withdrawn or dismissed. Though other for-profit colleges can be supportive, you still need to remain skeptical of their motives - don't forget that you'll be a rich profiteering thief, like so many other for-profit college owners.

Other major supports include shareholders of publicly traded for-profit colleges. Do a simple internet search for large for-profit colleges that are traded on the stock market. There are for-profit college companies that have market values in the millions and billions of dollars; and by the time you read this, some of these companies may have reached record values, all of which is federal funding converted to profit. Because the for-profit college industry is volatile, shares of these companies are rarely held as long term investments. These colleges are bought and sold quickly, making them loved by day traders and other investors interested in profiting from the exploitation of low-income borrowers.

Many traders and brokerage firms that hold for-profit college shares to offset risks don't know or care about the catastrophic student loan debts, increasing default rates, and low graduation rates. It's strictly business and trading. Technically, they're owners of these for-profit colleges, but only for the short-term. For-profit college students have no clue their college is being sold and bought daily, and they're especially unaware of being retained as a benefit to investors.

Another overlooked support to your business is a poor or depressed economy. As you're reading this, the economy is either doing well or it's not. Don't sweat it either way. You can still start the college and make a lot of profit. When the economy is tanking and people are losing their jobs, fear and desperation kick in; and that's when people start dreaming of a new path.

Most people don't prepare for their financial future. They live beyond their means and have no savings – these are great conditions for your Admissions Department to work its magic. Imagine a hard-working single mother living paycheck to paycheck or a poor immigrant who just lost two of his three jobs because of a down economy. These two potential customers can be easily pressured into returning to school or starting college courses for the first time, to gain additional skills and improve the likelihood of obtaining meaningful work when the economy rebounds. Bad economies are wonderful for for-profit colleges. A downturn in the economy is a prime time to snag many of the worried, fearful, and desperately unemployed adults. These victims are typically unaware of the pitfalls and trappings of for-profit colleges and student loans; thus, they are prone to believe the *dream* sales pitch from your Admissions Advisors.

At-risk customers who've been destroyed by a failing economy will be more likely to enroll online because of their age, as they believe the message they're too old to return to a traditional non-profit university - they imagine themselves sitting at desks surrounded by college kids, and don't want that experience. Nobody told them that many adults are returning to community colleges, receiving scholarships, and being educated through less expensive means. What they don't know hurts them, but profits you. Remember, ignorance equates to profit.

In a down economy, such as a recession, you may want to strengthen the Admissions Department. Hire more staff. Many of the people you hire onto Admissions teams will need a job, so they'll naturally know how to speak to your target population of jobless, and often homeless, adults. As mentioned previously, it's ideal to have Admissions Advisors match the target customer base.

Here's another secret to boosting your profits: Ensure your Admissions Advisors are in the same demographic, circumstances, and mindset as your prospective customers. When the economy takes a turn for the worst, you can easily hire more Admissions Advisors in dire straits, desperate for a job, and will vigilantly sell your fraudulent programs to similarly situated suckers.

Though a failing economy is a major support for your business, the biggest support may be in the Executive Branch of government. Depending on how the political winds are blowing, you might be lucky enough to start your for-profit college during an administration that favors avarice. You may even discover that an elective official owns, or once owned, a for-profit college. You'll be surprised. Don't think that everyone is opposed to a greedy entrepreneur with the ambition to steal Title IV and military funding. Some officials in the highest offices of government protect such rapacious drive and passion - to them, it's the ripest fruit of capitalism. If you're alive during an administration that favors the for-profit college mission, you would be crazy not to start a for-profit college.

Final Advice

By now you should feel better prepared to start your for-profit college without the restraints of a moral compass or the fear of being caught and investigated. If your college is investigated by the Department of Education, IRS, EEOC, SEC, or any other bureaucratic entity, you can follow your plan B. What is plan B you ask? Morph into a non-profit university!

You'll be wise to start a tax-exempt non-profit business on the side, or have someone elected to the Board of Trustees start one; that way, your for-profit college can be purchased and absorbed into the non-profit organization. There is so much confusion amongst bureaucracies as it is, regulators won't have a clue as to who should investigate such a brilliant maneuver. You'll be able to continue with the same scam, just disguised as a non-profit institution. Another plan is to simply place the college in teach-out mode, collect tuition and fees from the remaining students, and close the doors. You'll be so filthy rich at that point, it won't even matter.

Enjoy your for-profit college business and the lucrative wealth. By the way, take it easy on your butler and cook if they forget to greet you – they might be students at your college. If they're not, enroll them.

www.ingramcontent.com/pod-product-compliance
Lightning Source LLC
Chambersburg PA
CBHW032019170526
45157CB00002B/764